Alienation

INQUIRY INTO CRUCIAL AMERICAN PROBLEMS

Series Editor · JACK R. FRAENKEL

# Alienation:

## Individual or Social Problem?

*RONALD V. URICK*

Associate Professor of Education
Wayne State University

PRENTICE-HALL, INC.     ENGLEWOOD CLIFFS, N.J.

*Titles in this series:*

CRIME AND CRIMINALS: What Should We Do About Them?
Jack R. Fraenkel

PREJUDICE AND DISCRIMINATION: Can We Eliminate Them?
Fred R. Holmes

THE DRUG SCENE: Help or Hang-up?
Walter L. Way

POVERTY IN AN AFFLUENT SOCIETY: Personal Problem or National Disgrace?
David A. Durfee

COUNTRY, CONSCIENCE, AND CONSCRIPTION: Can They Be Reconciled?
Leo A. Bressler and Marion A. Bressler

VOICES OF DISSENT: Positive Good or Disruptive Evil?
Frank Kane

CITIES IN CRISIS: Decay or Renewal?
Rudie W. Tretten

TEEN-AGERS AND SEX: Revolution or Reaction?
Jack L. Nelson

PROPAGANDA, POLLS, AND PUBLIC OPINION: Are the People Manipulated?
Malcolm G. Mitchell

ALIENATION: Individual or Social Problem?
Ronald V. Urick

EDUCATION AND OPPORTUNITY: For What and For Whom?
Gordon M. Seely

FOREIGN POLICY: Intervention, Involvement, or Isolation?
Alvin Wolf

ISBN 0-13-022111-2 paper
ISBN 0-13-022129-5 cloth

1  2  3  4  5  6  7  8  9  10

Prentice-Hall International, Inc.,
*London*
Prentice-Hall of Australia, Pty. Ltd.,
*Sydney*
Prentice-Hall of Canada, Ltd.,
*Toronto*
Prentice-Hall of India Private Ltd.,
*New Delhi*
Prentice-Hall of Japan, Inc.,
*Tokyo*

# PREFACE

The series *INQUIRY INTO CRUCIAL AMERICAN PROB-LEMS* focuses upon a number of important contemporary social and political issues. Each book presents an in-depth study of a particular problem, selected because of its pressing intrusion into the minds and consciences of most Americans today. A major concern has been the desire to make the materials relevant to students. Every title in the series, therefore, has been selected because, in one way or another, it suggests a problem of concern to students today.

A number of divergent viewpoints, from a wide variety of different *kinds* of sources, encourage discussion and reflection and illustrate that the same problem may be viewed from many different vantage points. Of concern throughout is a desire to help students realize that honest men may legitimately differ in their views.

After a short chapter introducing the questions with which the book will deal, Chapter 2 presents a brief historical and contemporary background so that students will have more than just a superficial understanding of the problem under study. In the readings that follow, a conscientious effort has been made to avoid endorsing any one viewpoint as the "right" viewpoint, or to evaluate the arguments of particular individuals. No conclusions are drawn. Instead, a number of questions for discussion and reflection are posed at the end of each reading so that students can come to their own conclusions.

Great care has been taken to insure that the readings included in each book are just that—readable! We have searched particularly for articles that are of high interest, yet from which differing viewpoints may be legitimately inferred. Whenever possible, dialogues involving or descriptions showing actual people responding and reacting to problematic situations are presented. In sum, each book

- presents divergent, conflicting views on the problem under consideration;
- gives as many perspectives and dimensions on the problem as space permits;
- presents articles on a variety of reading levels, in order to appeal to students of many different ability levels;
- presents analytical as well as descriptive statements;
- deals with real people involved in situations of concern to them;
- includes questions which encourage discussion and thought of the various viewpoints expressed;
- includes activities to involve students to consider further the issues embedded in the problem.

# CONTENTS

**1** Introduction  1

1. She's Leaving Home  1
2. Detroit, Through a Bottle of Wine  2
3. Thirty-eight Witnesses  4

**2** What Is Alienation?  7

**3** Who Are the Alienated?  13

1. Art Johnston, Angry Young Man  13
2. Sunday Dinner in Brooklyn  17
3. John Sinclair, the Hippie Evangelist  23
4. The Problem That Has No Name  28
5. Wasteland  32
6. The Polite Fiction  33
7. The Exurbanite at Work  34
8. The Man on the Assembly Line  37
9. The Alienated Consumer  40
10. The Invisible Man  43
11. The Meaning of a "Conk"  44
12. Fifth Avenue, Uptown  46
13. The Alienated Voter  48

## 4 What Are the Alienating Pressures Today?  52

1. Poor Scholar's Soliloquy  52
2. Roots of Our Malady  55
3. I Am Waiting  58
4. Bureaucracy: The Impersonal Giant  62
5. The Great Emptiness  63
6. The Social Aspect of Work  67
7. Growing Up Black  69
8. Racial Disorder: Why Did It Happen?  72
9. The Permissive Society  75

## 5 How Can We Cope With Alienation?  79

1. When Silence Is a Crime  79
2. Can Parents Help?  83
3. Black Power  85
4. A Few Rays of Hope  90
5. A Piece of the Action  94
6. A Bill of Rights for Kids  96
7. I Care, You Care, He Cares  98
8. Columbia — The New America?  100
9. Participatory Democracy  103
10. Kilmer: Portrait of a Job Corps Center  106
11. To Save the Life of "I"  110

## Bibliography  115

# **1**

# Introduction

### 1. SHE'S LEAVING HOME *

Wednesday morning at five o'clock as the day begins
Silently closing her bedroom door
Leaving the note that she hoped would say more
She goes downstairs to the kitchen clutching her handkerchief
Quietly turning the backdoor key
Stepping outside she is free.
She (We gave her most of our lives)
is leaving (Sacrificed most of our lives)
home (We gave her everything money could buy)
She's leaving home after living alone
For so many years. Bye, bye
Father snores as his wife gets into her dressing gown
Picks up the letter that's lying there
Standing alone at the top of the stairs
She breaks down and cries to her husband
Daddy our baby's gone.
Why would she treat us so thoughtlessly
How could she do this to me.
She (We never thought of ourselves)
is leaving (Never a thought for ourselves)
home (We struggled hard all our lives to get by)
She's leaving home after living alone

---

For so many years. Bye, Bye
Friday morning at nine o'clock she is far away
Waiting to keep the appointment she made
Meeting a man from the motor trade.
She (What did we do that was wrong?)
is having (We didn't know it was wrong)
fun (Fun is the one thing that money can't buy)
Something inside that was always denied
For so many years. Bye, Bye
She's leaving home bye bye

## 2. DETROIT, THROUGH A BOTTLE OF WINE *

The stirrings of other "roomers" in the old, abandoned building woke me up. I was cold and stiff from sleeping on the hard, refuse-littered floor with nothing under or over me; I had bedded down with nothing but a "muscatel blanket." I grabbed for it and held it up to the dim light filtering in from somewhere, but it was empty. I put it to my lips anyway and drained the "spider," then threw it away.

In the gloom I could make out the forms of eight fellow lodgers. A few of them were having their eye-openers from jealously guarded bottles. I wanted to ask one of them for a drink but knew that it could be asking for a broken head. I kept my mouth shut.

A few of the bums had retreated to corners to heed the call of nature. No cheerful bantering. Each man lost in his own thoughts; each planning his day with the same meticulous attention to scheduling that the chairman of the board of a huge corporation might give to his affairs. Being a bum is not easy. Some were rolling up tattered blankets which they would surreptitiously stash when the others had gone. Several glanced at me, but none spoke.

It was still gray-early, but up-time for bums on Detroit's skid rows. Hit the streets to catch the working stiffs, and maybe panhandle a dime or two toward the day's first jug of wine. Beat the "Bum Squad" cops who prowl the streets in their unmarked cars looking for the winos, like me, to come out of the old buildings around dawn, like rats scuttling from a burning hole.

I had to have a drink.

I got to my feet and lurched toward the hole in the wall I'd come in through. Outside, a vacant lot; turn right, through a weedgrown tunnel, and onto the street. I walked south, shivering from the chill air, wonder-

---

* Excerpted from Ernest Chamberlain, "Detroit, Through a Bottle of Wine," *Detroit* Magazine, Detroit Free Press, September 8, 1968. Reprinted by permission of the author and the publisher.

ing what had happened to my jacket. Then I remembered; I had sold it for thirty-five cents. Small bottle.

I looked behind me. I looked across the street. I looked for a two block stretch ahead of me. I could see at least 50 wobbly, homeless figures coming out into the light of another day. Men without homes—or hope. Men without ambition beyond another drink. Men who were running from wives, homes, and children. From responsibility. From everything—and nothing. Running from themselves, mostly—as I was. Men who choose the ostrich-route; stick the head in a hole in the sand—the bottle—and though the prowling tiger's still out there, it can't be seen, therefore must not be real.

Skid Row. World of the lost and the damned.

I headed down Henry toward Woodward, to bum the price of a bottle of wine.

By seven A.M. the city was in full swing. The traffic was as thick as soldier ants on a troop movement, and just as determined. The sidewalks were filled with people: beautiful women, with freshly applied, glistening makeup, headed for their typewriters; men in Botany 500 and Hart-Shaffner-Marx slim looks; the lunch pail hordes in khaki pants and blue chambray shirts. The big green and yellow busses slamming to stops at the corners, leaving people and taking people, then roaring away, leaving noxious vapor trails. The late-to-work people and the pseudo-wealthy in their taxis.

And not too far away another skid-row derelict was about to die.

"Old John" was the only name I ever heard. He'd lost his right eye somewhere along the line of his miserable years. He never worked at anything, as far as anyone knew, and was a long-time Detroit bum. But his days of bumming and sub-animal living came to an abrupt end that morning in an alley just off Michigan Avenue. Heart attack? I never found out. He just dropped dead in the filth of the alley which was part of his home.

His body was still warm when the "hawks" swooped in. Three of them. Swiftly and silently they went through his pockets. One got a half-emptied sack of Bull Durham. Another yanked the shoes from Old John's feet. Then the three ghouls faded into nowhere again.

"Society" gave Old John a free burial—and he didn't have to bum it, either. . . .

Skid Row. Home of the oblivion-seekers. Drink the wine and escape the real world. No guts to kill the body, so kill the brain with alcohol. The wino bum is the stereotyped figure of the skid-row man all across America. With the picture goes the idea that there's not much the bum won't stoop to for a few pennies.

The image . . . is startlingly accurate.

\*      \*      \*      \*      \*

Self-imposed misery, degradation, living death, and finally the real McCoy, are skid row's only promise and fulfillment. Nothing else. It is, usually, a one-way tunnel.

### 3. THIRTY-EIGHT WITNESSES *

For more than half an hour thirty-eight respectable, law-abiding citizens in Queens watched a killer stalk and stab a woman in three separate attacks in Kew Gardens.

Twice the sound of their voices and the sudden glow of their bedroom lights interrupted him and frightened him off. Each time he returned, sought her out and stabbed her again. Not one person telephoned the police during the assault; one witness called after the woman was dead.

This is what the police say happened beginning at 3:20 A.M. in the staid, middle-class, tree-lined Austin Street area:

Twenty-eight-year-old Catherine Genovese, who was called Kitty by almost everyone in the neighborhood, was returning home from her job as manager of a bar in Hollis. She parked her red Fiat in a lot adjacent to the Kew Gardens Long Island Rail Road Station, facing Mowbray Place. Like many residents of the neighborhood, she had parked there day after day since her arrival from Connecticut a year ago, although the railroad frowns on the practice.

She turned off the lights of her car, locked the door and started to walk the 100 feet to the entrance of her apartment at 82-70 Austin Street, which is in a Tudor building, with stores on the first floor and apartments on the second.

The entrance to the apartment is in the rear of the building because the front is rented to retail stores. At night the quiet neighborhood is shrouded in the slumbering darkness that marks most residential areas.

Miss Genovese noticed a man at the far end of the lot, near a seven-story apartment house at 82-40 Austin Street. She halted. Then, nervously, she headed up Austin Street toward Lefferts Boulevard, where there is a call box to the 102d Police Precinct in nearby Richmond Hill.

She got as far as a street light in front of a bookstore before the man grabbed her. She screamed. Lights went on in the ten-story apartment house at 82-67 Austin Street, which faces the bookstore. Windows slid open and voices punctured the early-morning stillness.

Miss Genovese screamed: "Oh, my God, he stabbed me! Please help me! Please help me!"

---

* Excerpted from A. M. Rosenthal, *Thirty-Eight Witnesses.* © 1964 by The New York Times Company. Reprinted by permission.

From one of the upper windows in the apartment house, a man called down: "Let that girl alone!"

The assailant looked up at him, shrugged and walked down Austin Street toward a white sedan parked a short distance away. Miss Genovese struggled to her feet.

Lights went out. The killer returned to Miss Genovese, now trying to make her way around the side of the building by the parking lot to get to her apartment. The assailant stabbed her again.

"I'm dying!" she shrieked. "I'm dying!"

Windows were opened again, and lights went on in many apartments. The assailant got into his car and drove away. Miss Genovese staggered to her feet. A city bus, Q-10, the Lefferts Boulevard line to Kennedy International Airport, passed. It was 3:35 A.M.

The assailant returned. By then, Miss Genovese had crawled to the back of the building, where the freshly painted brown doors to the apartment house held out hope of safety. The killer tried the first door; she wasn't there. At the second door, 82-62 Austin Street, he saw her slumped on the floor at the foot of the stairs. He stabbed her a third time—fatally.

\*     \*     \*     \*     \*

The first attack came at 3:15. The first call to the police came at 3:50. Police arrived within two minutes, they say. Miss Genovese was dead.

That night and the next morning the police combed the neighborhood looking for witnesses. They found them, thirty-eight.

Two weeks later, when this newspaper heard of the story, a reporter went knocking, door to door, asking why, why.

Through half-opened doors, they told him. Most of them were neither defiant nor terribly embarrassed nor particularly ashamed. The underlying attitude, or explanation, seemed to be fear of involvement—any kind of involvement.

" I didn't want my husband to get involved," a housewife said.

"We thought it was a lovers' quarrel," said another woman. "I went back to bed."

"I was tired," said a man.

"I don't know," said another man.

"I don't know," said still another.

"I don't know," said others. . . .

---

Three very different situations, each evoking a different response as it is read—compassion for the skid row derelict; some sense of identification, perhaps, with the girl as she leaves home; indignation toward those people who appeared to turn their backs on their neighbor. But there is a common thread that runs through these stories, and it is with this thread that you will be concerned in this book.

In each of these cases a chasm, a wide gulf, exists between the persons involved. And this gulf—affecting, as it does, the ability of those persons to communicate with one another, to relate to one another, to "feel for" one another—is just one of a number of difficulties that confront many Americans in their relationships with each other, with the various institutions of our society, and with the society itself. These difficulties, grouped together and labelled *alienation,* are the focus of this book. As you read on, the following are some important questions about alienation that you may want to keep in mind:

1.  What do we mean by alienation?
2.  In what forms does alienation appear in our lives?
3.  Has alienation been a continuing human problem, or is it something new in America today?
4.  Who is alienated in America today?
5.  What does alienation "feel like"?
6.  How does alienation affect the way in which people live?
7.  What are the causes of alienation in our society?
8.  How can we learn to cope with the alienating pressures in our own lives?

The answers to these questions are many, varied, and, in some cases, conflicting. The material that follows will provide you with a basis for discussion and for reaching your own conclusions regarding the problem of alienation in American society today.

# What Is Alienation?

## Characteristics of Alienation

Alienation is a term that refers to certain perceptions and feelings that some people have about themselves and about one or more aspects of their social environment—as these two (self and environment) relate to one another. Roughly, these feelings and perceptions are the *reverse* of the view expressed by the English poet John Donne when he wrote:

No man is an island, entire of itself; every man is a piece of the continent, a part of the main; if a clod be washed away by the sea, Europe is the less, as well as if a promontory were, as if a manor of thy friends or of thine own were; any man's death diminishes me, because I am involved in Mankind; and therefore never send to know for whom the bell tolls; it tolls for thee.

The alienated individual may well see himself as an "island"—separated from his fellows, unattached to them, with few bonds or ties of any enduring or intimate nature. This sort of *social isolation*, then, we can speak of as one characteristic of alienation.

Now imagine yourself *on* an island in the middle of a large body of water and out of sight of any other land mass. If the day is bright and sunny, the horizon stands out sharply and it is very easy to distinguish the sea from the sky. If the day, however, is grey and overcast, the line of demarcation becomes so vague and ambiguous as to virtually disappear. As the bench marks, or points of contrast, that were available become no longer usable, your view tends, in a very real sense, to lose its meaning, and it becomes pointless to continue staring out to sea. Similarly, many people whom we could describe as alienated may feel that some aspects of their lives—or of the style of life around them—have no mean-

7

ing; it's a sort of "going through the motions" without any real point to it. This sense of *meaninglessness* about one's existence is another characteristic of alienation.

The disappearance of the "bench marks" that we referred to above suggests yet two more characteristics of alienation that will be helpful to keep in mind. Generally speaking, among groups of people living in association with one another there will be certain ways of behaving, of doing things, that are accepted by the members of the group. For these people, the patterns or standards (or bench marks) for living that they share are part of what holds them together. Social scientists generally refer to these standards or patterns as *norms*. In the alienated person, however (for reasons that we will explore in Chapter 4), there may be a loosening of the attachment to those norms, a feeling of separation from them, or an outright rejection of them. Feelings of *normlessness,* the absence of attachment to any definite set of standards, may characterize one who is alienated. So also may feelings of *estrangement* from the accepted norms indicate a sense of alienation.

Why doesn't a person who is suffering from these feelings *do* something about his life? The answer for the person who is alienated may be that he doesn't feel that there is anything he *can* do about it. The situation may appear to him to be outside his control and he feels "trapped," "hung-up," "in a rat race," "on a treadmill," or that "you can't fight city hall." This sense of lack of control over his destiny, this feeling of *powerlessness,* is another aspect of alienation.

Finally, if one feels socially isolated or estranged, if he has no strong attachments, if he views his life as essentially meaningless, if he sees himself as relatively unable to do anything about it—if one or more of these feelings are present—it becomes very difficult for him to answer the question, "Who am I?" A person's identity, his sense of who he is, derives from his relationships with others, particularly those people who are important to him. And so, a person whose relationships with those around him are viewed by him as empty or unclear, or for whom there is a clear estrangement or isolation of himself from others, may come increasingly to a state of self-estrangement. This condition, too, is a characteristic of the alienated individual.

We should be careful, however, as we discuss alienation, to avoid speaking of it in an absolute sense. That is, alienation is not an either-or proposition in the sense that someone is either pregnant or not pregnant. Alienation, since it is comprised of feelings and perceptions (which may vary in intensity) and since it involves social relationships (which vary in function as well as complexity) is better thought of as a combination of *degree* and *direction.* In a very rough way, then, we could speak of an individual (or group) as being *somewhat* alienated or *very* alienated (thus indicating degree) *toward* or *with respect to* (thus indicating direction) some aspect or aspects of their lives. As you read in Chapter 3 about some of the alienated groups in American society, you will have an opportunity to explore the questions of degree and direction of alienation as well as identify the several characteristics of alienation "in action." Before turning to that, however, it would be well to take a quick look at alienation from an historical view.

## Alienation in the Past

Alienation has been a fact of existence for a number of individuals and groups down through history. Imagine yourself, for example, a black African in the 1600's and 1700's, who is wrenched from his homeland, loaded onto ships, and brought to the New World. You are separated from your family and friends, removed from all connection with your culture and traditions, thrust into a totally new environment, and required to do strange and tiring work for men whose relationship to you is that of a property owner and from whom there is virtually no escape except through death. It is not hard to see that your feelings—and those of many of your fellow slaves—would involve a large measure of alienation.

Or think of Martin Luther. Raised in a deeply religious family, in a religiously homogeneous community, and at a time when religion was an extremely important part of the culture, Martin Luther grew into a life of dedication and commitment to the service of his church. What sort of feelings do you suppose Martin Luther experienced, when as a consequence of his dedication, commitment, and study, he was forced to break with his church, his culture, and his tradition? How did he feel when he nailed his ninety-five theses to the door of the church and said, "Here I stand; I can do no other "?

The stories of some of the more famous migrations of groups of people in the past also carry evidence that the existence of alienated feelings and perceptions were part of the conditions that led to the decision to pull up stakes and try to build a new life in another place. The most familiar, perhaps, of these stories is that of the Pilgrims. Viewed as outcasts by the dominant groups of English society and finding the practice of their religion harassed and obstructed, a number of these Separatists (as they were called) decided to move to the more tolerant climate across the English Channel in Holland. While their religious needs were thus largely satisfied, these people found the customs and traditions of the Dutch strange and uncomfortable, and they sensed a growing estrangement between themselves and their children. It was then that a group of the Pilgrims decided to venture to the New World.

The theme of alienation, moreover, runs through a large body of religious, mythological, and literary expressions stretching back almost to the beginnings of the written word. The Old Testament, for example, is replete with stories of alienation, from the separation of Adam and Eve from God as it is described in Genesis, through the wanderings of the Israelites, to the stories of the prophets in the latter books of the Old Testament. Similarly, in the myths of ancient Greece and in the work of a number of ancient Greek dramatists and poets are found the themes of isolation and estrangement and of powerlessness in the face of one's fate. The same point could be made about several of Shakespeare's plays, and it would be interesting to view Hawthorne's *The Scarlet Letter* or Mark Twain's *Tom Sawyer* from the standpoint of alienation. There are, of course, many other illustrations and examples that could be mentioned here. Perhaps you can think of some from your own reading.

In any case, since writers draw primarily on their own experiences and observations, we can conclude that when the theme of alienation appears as part of the literature of an era or culture, we will find instances of alienation occurring in the life of that era or culture.

### Alienation in Modern America

One of the interesting things to notice, however, about the instances of alienation that we mentioned above is that they are all situations in which individuals or groups chose to move or were forced to exist outside of the mainstream of that society. The slaves, for example, though *in* American society, were certainly not *part of it,* at least in any meaningful sense.

Looking back on Martin Luther's action from the vantage point of today makes it possible to see that this action heralded the beginning of a different "mainstream" from the one that existed in his time. Yet there can be little doubt that the steps that he felt compelled to take were away from several of the major social and cultural traditions of the age. And, finally, though the conditions of life for the Separatists in England in the early 1600's were alienating, they were largely the result of repressive and coercive actions taken by British officialdom.

The point is that in none of these cases can it be said that *alienation per se* was a major problem confronting that society. And it is this issue that is being raised by a large number of writers as they look at American society today. That is to say, many scholars, social scientists, poets, novelists, and others who are concerned with social and interpersonal relationships, have come to believe that alienated feelings and perceptions are spread widely throughout our population. Some of these students of American society would go so far as to assert that alienation is a characteristic of life in America today.

There is some evidence that our current situation is not a completely unique one. Eric and Mary Josephson have written:

In its panorama of disorder and change, history offers plentiful evidence that men in times past also felt no small uncertainty about themselves and their identities, suffered no little anguish of gloom, despair and feelings of detachment from each other. Karl Jaspers quotes an Egyptian chronicler of four thousand years ago: "Robbers abound. . . . No one ploughs the land. People are saying: 'We do not know what will happen from day to day.' . . . dirt prevails everywhere, and no longer does any one wear clean raiment. . . . The country is spinning round and round like a potter's wheel. . . . Slave-women are wearing necklaces of gold and lapis lazuli. . . . No more do we hear any one laugh. . . . Great men and small agree in saying: 'Would that I had never been born.' . . . No public office stands open where it should, and the masses are like timid sheep without a shepherd. . . . Artists have ceased to ply their art. . . . The few slay the many. . . . One who yesterday was indigent is now wealthy, and the sometime rich overwhelm him with adulation. . . . Impudence is rife. . . . Oh that man could cease to be, that women should no longer conceive and give birth. Then, at length, the world would find peace." [1]

Thucydides describes a similar moral collapse in Greece during the Peloponnesian War. As for medieval Europe, Huizinga reminds us that the Middle Ages were essentially violent in character: wars, class struggles, hysterical crowd behavior, vice and crime (on an unparalleled scale, particularly in university towns), plagues, scarcity, superstition, the conviction that the world was coming to an end—such was the "black" background of medieval life. A late medieval (fifteenth-century) French poet, Eustache Deschamps, cried:

> Why are the times so dark
> Men know each other not at all,
> But governments quite clearly change
> From bad to worse?
> Days dead and gone were more worth while,
> Now what holds sway? Deep gloom and boredom,
> Justice and law nowhere to be found.
> I know no more where I belong.

But the America of today is not 15th Century Europe or Greece in 400 B.C., and it certainly is not the Egypt of two thousand years before

---

[1] Reprinted from *Man Alone: Alienation in Modern Society,* edited, with an Introduction, by Eric and Mary Josephson. Copyright © 1962 by Dell Publishing Co., Inc. and used by permission of the publisher.

Christ. And there is little consolation, if we live in an Age of Alienation, in knowing that there have been others before us. For we live in the *present,* not the past; and the accommodations we make, the courses of action we choose, and the lives we live must be in *our* situation rather than that of men who have long since passed from the scene. It is of these things that the history of America in the last half of the twentieth century will be written.

---

**What Do You Think?**

1. Do you consider the problem of alienation to be a psychological one or a social one? Might there be other ways of viewing it? Explain.

2. Some people might react to the characterization of American society as being beset with alienation by saying, "So what?" What consequences do you think there might be for a society in which alienation, as we have defined it, is widespread? What evidence can you offer to support your view?

3. In what ways is life today different from life in the 1400's? Similar? How are these differences and similarities relevant for considering alienation as a social problem?

# Who Are the Alienated?

Who is alienated in modern America? What does being alienated feel like? How do these feelings affect the lives of the people who are alienated? In this chapter you will have an opportunity to formulate some answers to these questions.

## 1. ART JOHNSTON, ANGRY YOUNG MAN *

*Art Johnston, the subject of the following article, is a "young American." So are you. As you read, compare your feelings with those expressed by Art to the author of the article.*

What the hell happened? One minute the kids were cute, vacuous, All-American and the next minute—it all happened in the blink of an eye—something clicked, and it was no longer football jerseys and proms, not by a long shot, brother, but where were you? Not to have noticed when it happened?

Talk to them; they will cut out your hopeful heart with their quick tongues, a slicing upward glance; they know. They are not children nor adolescents nor adults, no, they are something new, God's truth, something altogether original and unexpected. Whether they will endure is the big question, but you cannot deny that they have shaken off some of the old ways of looking and thinking and talking and being and now they are making up their own new ways.

---

* Excerpted from John Askins, "Art Johnston, Angry Young Man," *Detroit* Magazine, Detroit Free Press, October 6, 1968. Reprinted by permission of the author and the publisher.

Art Johnston, 24. "The hippie is willing to defy American society openly, you know?" Art's eyes glow, and so does his voice. "The hippie is willing to stand off from American society and say, 'American society, I scorn you. I scorn everything you stand for.' And truly be, you know, like a prophet in the wilderness."

Now if you want to hear something capable of making the chills run along your back, the vibrant exultation of Art's voice when he says those words will do nicely. Can such words come out joyful from a 24-year-old formerly middle-class mouth? They do.

Art is not a hippie; he is simply saying he digs their defiance. Art is just a young man with a beard. He was until recently a student at Wayne State and editor of the student newspaper, The South End. His newspaper was hostile to anything it considered authoritarian, phoney or unjust, and so is Art.

He is usually dressed in motorcycle boots, Levis, a broad belt, wildly colored shirt, silver medallion hanging from his neck on a leather string, unruly hair and, of course, the beard. Not long, but awfully defiant looking.

Why is it that both young rebels and advertising executives wear beards these days? Art says he wears one because "first of all you are setting yourself off, you are letting people know who you are. And I also perceive it as a screen, because it will screen people out whom you wouldn't want anything to do with anyway.

"Then there's the sexuality of hair. There's something almost obscene about a beard. Wearing your hair short and being clean-shaven is a symbol of civilization, of being civilized."

Very civilized ad men wear their beards for somewhat similar reasons, but their beards are controlled, well-tended, conservative, urbane. Art's is just hostile. He explains: "I was a rebel from the Boy Scouts. I got kicked out of the altar boys. All the way through. I was kicked out of a high school, expelled from a university. I was always, you know, questioning. Always let's say radical in the questions I'd ask. I was always very individual. And then there was this whole thing about authority.

"I ran away when I was 16, after I got kicked out of school, and I lived in Florida about four months. Finally I was caught in Arizona. After that I spent the major part of two summers just on the road, you know, and before I was 21 there were two or three years I'd just work and travel and float, more or less.

"Finally I got married and settled down. The marriage, you know, really settled me down and helped me; relating to someone really helped settle me down. I tried to go to work for General Motors. For a couple of years I worked for them up the street here, and I tried to convince myself that I was going to really settle down and be, you know, responsible; business, wife, and all that sort of stuff.

"I was a sort of assistant flunky to the executives, a very easy job. In fact, I only worked about an hour a day and I spent the rest of the time reading. Well, after reading for two years I became so—it was an intellectual reaction to the whole thing—I thought, 'I just can't stay around this place.'

"As far as I was concerned, the executives who were supposed to be important were just concerning themselves with trivia. And talk about escape, I really thought they were escaping. These trivial things which they thought were so important! And I just had to leave, and I came back to the university."

He speaks in a torrent of words. You have to think quickly to keep up with him. His body lounges but his blue eyes are intense. He is compressed, controlled. So long as he trusts you he will be open and honest; cross him and he will cut you down without blinking. At least, that is the impression you get.

He is 24 and uncertain about the future, what to do with it. "It's something I worry about every night," he said a few months ago. "I don't know what the hell I'm going to do when I get out of school. I could put it off a couple more years by going to grad school, but it really is a hangup." He solved his problem at least temporarily last month when he decided suddenly to leave school.

He abandoned General Motors for the university, but authority was there too, waiting for him. Now he has left. In the interim he was among other things, editor of The South End. The South End had its critics and its faults, but its circulation rose from 12,000 to 18,000 during Art's tenure and Nat Hentoff, the Village Voice columnist, named it the nation's best college newspaper for 1967. It was an impressive indication of what Art could do with a job he considered worthwhile.

"We're splitting now," he wrote in a farewell editorial. "We didn't quite get our certificate diploma accreditation passport. Guess we'll never get that 'good job' now. (Refrains of our collective childhood: 'Do you want to work in a factory all your life?') But we want something else, and we want it bad. We want to be free.

"Free from someone else—or even everybody else—dictating what we should think, the way we should live, the questions we should ask, and even the way we should dream (hope). We want to be free from the overwhelming finality of a society that lives the mass hallucination of freedom, when all our lives have been programmed and projected, and all that remains is filling in the names, the dates, and the titles of the institutions. We want to be free of the certainty of the future."

He is contradictory, you see. "It's something I worry about every night . . . we want to be free of the certainty of the future."

When he was still in school, he said once: "It's very funny that just about every day I run into somebody who tries to tell me that after I get out of school I'll adopt all the right things, all the right customs, and be concerned with suburbia and all that stuff.

"And I wonder, why do these people keep asking me about that? And sometimes I think it's a sort of guilt, like these people were rebels themselves when they were young and they sort of hope I'll settle down too so they won't have to feel guilty about themselves now."

But Art has disappointed them. After quitting school he worked for a time on the Fifth Estate, the local underground newspaper, and he didn't shave his beard or anything. Then in July he just—left. Set out for California on his motorcycle, a friend says.

"We're leaving," he wrote in that farewell editorial. "Maybe we've been here long enough. Maybe it's the summer. Maybe it's the grumble of a '49 Harley Davidson, impatient to have its chrome stripped, and its engine bored. Maybe we'll see you somewhere else. Maybe California. Maybe on the highway."

The highway . . . California . . . roaring through darkness, past empty filling stations, through silent small towns . . . alone . . . . A vision of the ultimate modern hero: a man alone and apart, moving to his destiny, buffeted by wind and rain and time but unbowed.

Heroic. There is a basic hunger in most people to believe their lives are in some way heroic, in some way meaningful . . . But reality points us more and more the other way, these days. At home, at work, in the supermarket, on the street, everything is taken care of, neatly prepackaged, and there are very few decisions left to make, very few risks to take.

Art Johnston is a rebel against all that. His rebellion is simple fury at the forces which would chain him to the earth when all his senses insist he was meant to be an eagle. He is no freak. Less desperate people turn to alcohol, to fast sporty cars, to sex, to drugs, to crime, to gambling. They are called maladjusted or neurotic or sophisticated, but in fact they are afflicted with the great malady of our times. It is called boredom.

---

**What Do You Think?**

1.   How would you characterize Art's feelings toward America? Refer to statements in the article to support your view.

2.   If you were in a "bull session" with Art, how would you respond to him? What do you think he would say to you in return?

## 2. SUNDAY DINNER IN BROOKLYN *

*In the following short story, another young American tells of his experience in returning home for a visit with his mother and father.*

The subway's roaring and screaming in the darkness, the passing under the river with the pressure in my ears—these were such a classical overture to going back home that I was weary of the joke. Riding the wrong way like that, I felt I had left Brooklyn for Manhattan only to discover on arriving that I had forgotten something I needed. Now, retracing my steps, I found the ride an endless torture, as it always inexplicably is under these circumstances, although when I was going in the other direction the distance passed unnoticed.

Of course it was my mother and father I'd forgotten, and I'd do it all over again next time too, but by now I accepted this as in the nature of things. They could hardly forget me though, because they had my picture on the mantle next to the clock. It was ten years old, that picture, but they never asked for a new one, and I was convinced that this was the way they still saw me. Like a criminal, I might alter my appearance, but they were not to be fooled. Each time I arrived, I could see their moist eyes washing away my disguise.

I was holding a book open on my lap—I always carried a book to Brooklyn, as an amulet or charm, a definition of my delicate ego—but for all the reading I did I might just as well have put it into the seat of my pants. My mind kept dropping down the page like a marble in a pinball machine until I finally gave it up, conceding that no book could successfully compete with my favorite fiction, my mother and father.

\*     \*     \*     \*     \*

[When] I saw the name of my own station through the open door and I jumped up and ran through it barely in time, . . .

At the top of the stairs the sun hit me in the eye. It seemed to me that the sun was always shining in Brooklyn, drying clothes, curing rickets, evaporating puddles, inviting children out to play, and encouraging artificial-looking flowers in front yards. Against my will, it warmed over an ineffable melancholy in me. I felt that it was a great democratic source of central heating for this big house in which everyone lived together.

\*     \*     \*     \*     \*

---

* Excerpted from Anatole Broyard, "Sunday Dinner in Brooklyn," *Partisan Review,* from Avon Book of Modern Writing, Avon Books, 1954. © Anatole Broyard.

The scene was made even more sententious by the fact that it was Sunday. There was a tremendous vacuum left behind by God. In contrast to the kitchenlike intimacy of the church on Thompson Street—which in its ugliness succeeded in projecting its flock's image on the universe—the spiky shells on these blocks had a cold, punitive look, and seemed empty except for those few hours in the morning when people came with neutralized faces to pay their respects to a dead and departed deity.

From the corner, I could see my mother in the front yard. Her face was turned toward me, although I knew she couldn't see me at that distance. I had the feeling that wherever I was, her face was always turned toward me. Now she saw me, she was waving and talking. In a moment she would begin to shout. I was already smiling and gesticulating too. I modified my walk, making it playful. "Hello, Paul!" she was shouting. "How are you?" I was still too far to talk. I wanted to run, I always wanted to run those last few yards. I hated the last few steps, the final enormous gap, between us. Once we were close enough, like lovers in embrace, we wouldn't be able to see each other so clearly.

I seized her by the shoulders and bent to kiss her. As usual, each of us offered a cheek. Quickly we turned our heads, and somehow miraculously avoided kissing each other on the lips, our heads turning just far enough so that each kissed the other with half a mouth in the middle of the cheek, making three or four smacks for good measure. My father was inside. He would have liked to come out too, but he felt he would be a spectacle, and besides he seemed to think that she ought to greet me alone, as though she were giving birth to me again.

He met me at the doorway, and we clogged up there, gesticulating and embracing. We always gesticulated too much, we distrusted language and thoughts. And all the while we were shouting, as if we were singing an opera. "Take off your coat!" they were shouting. "Take off your tie!" Sometimes I almost expected them to ask for my belt and shoelaces, but I suppose they knew that, after all, there was no way of disarming the dagger of the mind.

"Wait, I'll make you a martini!" my father shouted, and he ran off into the kitchen. "Sit down!" my mother shouted. "Make yourself comfortable!" Shoving me into my father's chair, she pressed the button on the arm and I was suddenly in a horizontal position. She switched the radio to WQXR, and one of the more familiar symphonies poured out like coal out of a chute.

This chair had been a gift to my father on one of his birthdays. My mother was delighted by the idea of the button. I never liked it. It always struck me as uncanny. I felt myself straining in it, trying to keep my head up a little. My father came in with the martini. I saw that it was amber. He never thought to make himself one. Like a servant.

The martini was sweet. Suddenly I realized that I loved them very much. But what was I going to do with them?

"Here's the Book Review," my mother said, handing me the paper. They both sat down, waiting for me to read it. How could I read it with them sitting there watching me as if I were performing a great feat? I was a spectacle, they assumed I didn't want to talk to them. I understood too that, in a way, they liked to believe I wasn't there just for a visit, and it was perfectly natural for me to be reading the Book Review of a Sunday afternoon.

I put the paper down, reassuring them that I'd read it later. We looked at each other for a moment, smiling. I felt that I was stretched out on a bier. Pressing the button, I allowed the back of the chair to come up. I smiled at my mother to show her I didn't mind the chair. I liked it, but I just felt like sitting up, I was such a bundle of energy.

"Well, how's everything, Paul?" she said. From the time I had been two years old, they had called me Bud, but somewhere in the last few years they began calling me Paul the way the outside world did. "Everything's fine," I said, realizing of course that they had no idea what that everything embodied. This vagueness was our tenderness. They'd have loved to know, but they were afraid of finding out something which might have offended not them, but me.

The dinner was ready. It was always ready when I arrived. Sometimes I had the fantasy of just walking by the house: my mother would be in the front yard, holding a box lunch in her hands. I would take the box without stopping. My face would be expressionless, hers grieving but controlled. My father would stand just inside the doorway . . .

My mother brought in the roast and my father carved it with great concentration, as if he were carving out our destiny. He placed on my plate the portion he had always desired for me. My mother heaped potatoes, gravy, vegetables on my plate. "I know you like to eat," she said, smiling and heaping my plate still more. This was a fiction. I never ate heartily, but nevertheless I exclaimed, "You know me, Mom!"

Pretending I could scarcely wait, I attacked the roast with knife and fork, while my mother held back to observe this. "Home cooking," I mumbled around a mouthful, these two words speaking volumes to her. I wondered what she thought I ate every day, whether she ever speculated for a moment that I might have liked it better. As a matter of history, the first time I ate in the Automat, when I was about twelve, I discovered that my mother was not an especially good cook, and this had hurt me as much as anything in my childhood. I could hardly swallow the food for years after that, but practice makes perfect, and I had learned to chomp with the histrionic absorption of a movie hero on a picnic.

As we ate, we regressed in time, reingesting all the events that had separated us. We retraced our steps to the very beginning, and there, joining hands, we advanced again from the birth of the soft-eyed boy to my embarrassing and unassimilable prodigality there at the table. To their great surprise, it always came out the same. We always bumped up against the present. Each time we raised our eyes from the plate, we were startled to discover each other, so camouflaged by time. As soon as our eyes met, we jumped back, as from an abyss. In these encounters, we resembled two forever inhibited people who press against each other in the subway: both want the contact, but neither dares admit it. . . .

Our conversation consisted of answerable questions and unquestionable answers. As usual, my mother found that I looked thin. All my life, I had managed to stay thin as a reproach to her, and on her side, as if a mother's role were that of a fanatic taxidermist, she had done her best to stuff me. She asked me where I took my laundry. "Aren't the prices outrageous? And the way they boil your clothes in all that acid, a shirt doesn't last six months." She was working around to suggesting that I bring my laundry to her. Maybe those dirty shirts would tell her what she was so anxious, and so ashamed, to know. A smear of lipstick, a smell, a stain, might paint a Japanese picture.

My father discussed the last month's boxing matches. Since I occasionally watched televised bouts in a bar, this had become a regular gambit. With an old man's memory, which clings to things as a child clings to its mother, for fear of being abandoned, he recalled every blow. If I happened to disagree with him—by mistake, or because I wasn't following him—he revised his version accordingly. We fought those fights side by side.

When he wasn't talking about boxing, his remarks were designed to show me that he was a liberal, a man who understands. Yesterday he gave up his seat in the subway to a Negress. Jews are smart. Everybody does things without knowing why. Nobody can say who's right and who's wrong. There are two sides to every question.

I remembered him when he was ten feet tall and his every statement was revelation of the absolute order of things. I tried to steer him around to himself, to push him gently back into his own indistinctly remembered convictions, but this only succeeded in panicking him. He tried to believe that the only difference between us was that I was "modern." He was going to be "modern" too, by denying everything he felt, and forgetting the few lessons life had taught him. He thought of my modernity as relentless and inescapable, a march of history which would let nothing —parents least of all—stand in its way.

My mother was smiling, and as I watched her over a forkful of mashed potatoes I realized that she was still pretty. I knew that smile from way back, I remembered how it had once outshone the sun in heaven.

Only, it had had more of a Mona Lisa character than, an ambiguity that gave it a special quality of romance. Where was that romance now? I wondered. Which of us was unfaithful, and why? Each was caricatured by a love we didn't know how to express. Afraid to feel, we were condemned to think, and at the same time not to think. When—and how—had our oneness become three? What ingredient was added to my mixture to turn it to poison? What alchemy isolated my substance beyond their—and my—understanding? There we were, playing a painful game of blindman's buff. We began by bandaging our eyes; then the bandages had fallen away and we had realized that we were blind.

At last I judged that I had eaten enough, an exemplary amount. With all my blood and nerves busy in my stomach, I relaxed, I became flatulent with affection. My mother saw my face go blank and she beamed. Belly to belly, that was the only true way to talk.

My father was describing how, on the job, he had solved a problem that had stumped even the architect. He had just 'scribed a plumb line on the floor. "Well I'll be god-damned," the architect had said, "if old Pete hasn't gone and done it again!" As I listened to this story, I never doubted it for a moment, and I was proud of him. . . .

My father was still talking about the job. He seemed very proud to have a hand in this particular building, which had been given a lot of publicity and which was apparently expected to become a world-famous monument on Broadway. As superintendent, he had a set of plans, and he brought them out for me to see. I recognized the name of a large low-priced clothing chain which sold standard stuff on installments. Feigning a show of interest, I studied the plans. Besides some very ill-adapted functionalist architecture, the building boasted two tremendous figures—a male and a female nude—above its facade, on either side of the store name like parentheses. They were over fifty feet high, my father assured me, and would be draped in neon lights. "They're like the Statue of Liberty on Broadway," he said, and I knew by the tone of his voice that he was quoting somebody. "What are they supposed to stand for?" I asked, in spite of the feeling I had that this question was all wrong. He looked at me, surprised and a little embarrassed. He was searching his mind for an answer, and although by now I didn't want an answer, I didn't know how to stop what I had started. I looked at the plans again. The figures were sexless, without even the pretense of drapery or a fig leaf. I knew what they stood for. The Statue of Liberty, since it was a French gift, may be presumed to have something under her robes, but these were American-made, this was the naked truth.

My father moved his lips as if to speak, but said nothing. In spite of myself again, I turned on him inquiringly, and he dropped his eyes. "It seems like a mighty big job, Pop," I said. "They must have a lot of confidence in you." "You said a mouthful," he said quickly, plainly relieved. "The architect himself asked for me."

*     *     *     *     *

Suddenly I felt a mushrooming urge to blurt out something—I don't know what—"I think you're great, Pop," or "I'm with you," or "To hell with them all," and this made me very nervous, so nervous I could hardly sit still. In desperation, I abruptly decided to leave. With my mouth still full of lemon meringue pie, I announced apologetically that I had an unbreakable appointment for which I was already late. I had been on the point of calling them up, I improvised, for that very reason, but I felt that even a short visit was better than none. I would come again soon and we would have a nice long talk.

They immediately fell into a frenzy of reassurances. Talking both at once, drowning each other out, they assured me that I didn't have to give explanations to them, they certainly understood how busy I was, and they had not the most infinitesimal wish to interfere with these quintessential commitments. Perish the thought—perish, in fact, the mother and father who would interrupt for a thousandth of a second their son's glorious onrush toward his entelechy.[3] . . .

Caught up in their extravagance, I reiterated my determination to come again soon with all the fervor of MacArthur vowing to return to the Philippines. I again congratulated my mother for having served up a truly historic feast and made ready to leave, avoiding my own eyes in the mirror as I knotted my tie.

My father left the room for a moment and reappeared in his coat. He would walk me to the subway, he said. I was on the point of protesting, but I knew I shouldn't, so I said "O.K., Pop, let's go." I kissed my mother, and she walked out to the gate with us.

Closing the gate behind me, I said, "So long, Mom," and she answered, "So long, Bud," slipping unconsciously into my old nickname again. The sound of it moved me more than I would have thought possible, and I impulsively kissed her again before my father and I faded from her sight.

At the corner I looked back to see her still standing there, her features erased by distance, and I waved, although I knew she couldn't see me. To my astonishment, she waved back. I caught the movement of her arm in the corner of my eye just as I was turning my head. I couldn't believe I had actually seen it—I knew she couldn't see across the street without her glasses. I stopped and took a step back—she was gone. Had I imagined it? It seemed very important to me to find out, and then I realized that I believed she *knew* when I turned the corner, she *sensed*

---

[1] Self-realization. A vital force directing growth.

it. No, no, I expostulated with myself, she only knew how long it took us to reach the corner, and then she waved. . . .

"What's the matter?" It was my father, asking why I had stopped. "I was wondering how Mom could see this far," I said. "She just waved at us." "Yeah, she waves three, four times," he said indifferently, and we started off toward the subway again. . . .

We had reached the subway entrance and I stopped, but he began to descend the steps. I seized him by the arm. "You don't have to walk me down, Pop," I said.

He was surprised. "That's all right," he said. "I haven't got anything else to do."

"Yeah, but what's the use of your breathing all those fumes and then having to come all the way up again?" I said, still holding his arm.

He was disappointed, I could see that he wanted to walk me down. "O.K., Pop," I said, letting go of his arm and starting down, "I guess a few steps don't faze you, do they?"

"No," he said, "I'm used to them," and we went down together and he came back up alone.

---

**What Do You Think?**

1.  How would you describe Paul's relationship with his parents?
2.  How would you compare Paul's feelings with the feelings of the girl described in the Beatles' song, "She's Leaving Home," which you read in Chapter I? With Art Johnston's feelings? With your own feelings?

### 3.  JOHN SINCLAIR, THE HIPPIE EVANGELIST * ‹

*John Sinclair, about whom you will read in the following article, represents another direction taken by many young people who have become disaffected with their lives.*

John Sinclair is an evangelist whom people call a hippie. He is trying, by example, to show the rest of society how it ought to live. John is sometimes discouraged because television and newspapers and magazines distort hippie life. "People don't have any idea of what we do," he complains.

---

* Excerpted from John Askins, "John Sinclair, the Hippie Evangelist," *Detroit Magazine*, Detroit Free Press, October 6, 1968.

The hippie movement, as presented by the mass media, is reportedly dying or dead on the East and West Coasts, and it suffered a sharp setback in Detroit when Sinclair and about 20 other hippies packed up and moved to Ann Arbor in July, grumbling about the five-day curfew that followed the assassination of Martin Luther King, Jr. Even the term "hippie" has fallen into disrepute, the preferred term being "the liberated sector," Sinclair says. But though the media's hippie movement may be dying, John Sinclair is alive and well.

He is a big, shaggy, gentle-voiced bear who sometimes finds it difficult to explain what the liberated sector is up to. But he tries. "It's kinda hard to describe in its own terms. But compared to the kind of scene that most of us come out of—you know, white, middle class suburban homes . . ."

John has his own home now, a rambling old house of 18 rooms, and his family includes a wife, a baby daughter, and 15–20 other hippies who live in the house or two other houses next door. Plus innumerable cats and kittens. There are two rock bands and a psychedelic light show and the family sells homemade posters, beads and books of poetry. Everyone contributes to the common good, commune-style, and the family does well. The houses rent for a total of $550 a month, there are three new panel trucks for the bands and an elaborate sound system for concerts. "We work harder than your average hippie," Sinclair says.

When they were in Detroit, he and his friends spent much of their spare time explaining themselves to suburban clubs and other civic gatherings of the square world. "We let them ask questions and we tried to answer them honestly," he says. "But usually they asked the wrong questions."

Why did those suburbanites care? Obviously, the liberated sector disturbed them. Why did the hippies bother? John Sinclair the Evangelist explains:

"People think that everything is relative, that our way of living or their way is just a matter of taste. But the fact is that there are healthy ways of living and unhealthy ways of living, and no amount of opinions or learned dissertations is going to make an unviable life form viable. People weren't made to be robots.

"The general cultural values in this country have evolved to a stage where they have to do entirely with products and jobs. If you don't have a job then you aren't a human being.

"A job means that you work from eight to five and you get a paycheck every Friday and you have payments to make, and if you don't have that then you're a nigger or a degenerate or a drag on the economy. And that's very weird. Especially when we're at a time right now when only a very small percentage of the population actually has to work.

"People really get uptight if you tell them they don't have to work:

'Well what would we DO?' They don't know how to read, they don't know how to listen to music, they don't know how to touch each other . . ."

As he talks, his wife, Magdalene, brings him breakfast; poached egg on toast and a glass of milk. She brings a glass of orange juice for a visitor. The baby she was carrying around earlier has been tucked away for a moment. She is shy and pretty and dressed like any suburban housewife in slacks and a sweater.

In 1966, Sinclair was sent to jail for six months for possession of marijuana. He celebrated his first wedding anniversary behind bars. When he got out, he wrote a poem to the detective who arrested him. It reads at one point:

> Come on out of that jail, Warner,
> let your criminals go, you've just trapped them
> in your silly bag, & there's no need for those games,
> we're all lovely & free Warner;
> we're all human beings, & nothing you can do
> can ever change the universe—

Elsewhere, he asks the detective what will happen

> when you have to try to arrest
> all the people younger than I am
> who smoke marijuana every day
> & don't even care about you at all, when you come to bust them
> all they'll do is laugh in your face, you're so funny, you come on
> like someone on your tv set . . .

Now Sinclair faces another marijuana charge, and this one could mean 20 years to life if he is convicted. But John refuses to worry. Meanwhile, what *will* the law do about all those kids, the teenyboppers who imitate the liberated sector not only in drugs but also in dress, hair styles, beards, irreverence toward the consumer economy and free experimentation with sex?

"They found out that all the crap their mothers told them just wasn't true," Sinclair says, "that there just wasn't any reason for them not to make love to each other."

Most persons will not be happy at the thought of their children seeking Sinclair out, listening to his advice, yet that is what happens. But then, Sinclair is willing to talk, and listen.

"I'm in Detroit at the Grande Ballroom and all these freaky kids are out there and they're just having a great time," he says. "They got beautiful clothes on and their hair is blowing in the wind, and the thing I always think is like they all gotta go home to their parents and go in their bedrooms and get hollered at because they were out until one o'clock.

You know, like what's gonna happen? We saw an indication of it when the schools got out last summer and huge waves of kids just headed for San Francisco because, you know, that was where it was AT, and they really wanted to find out where it was at."

The Grande (pronounced "grandie") Ballroom was once the site of stately waltzes and high-priority social affairs, but the neighborhood around Grand River and Beverly (one block south of Joy, the posters promise) has changed with the times and the debutantes are gone. Nonetheless, it is possible still to dance at the Grande. You must be over 17 and it is best to understand from the start that the music gets a bit loud.

It is Friday night at the Grande and 2,000 youngsters plus a few older hippies have poured in at $4 a head to see The Who, dance, be together and lose themselves in the mind-shattering orgy of light and sound. This is where it is at. A fire truck screams to a stop outside, siren howling, lights flashing, the whole bit, for a car is afire nearby. The celebrants inside do not notice.

Despite the noise there is some communication. Looks suffice when they dance, a hand around the waist when they stand and watch. Talking might be a hindrance anyway. Occasionally a hand slips down to rest casually but explicitly on a bottom, but no one pays much attention. To do so would be uncool.

For others there is no communication. They may dance but their eyes look inward and it is impossible to pick out their partners. Or they walk around and around the dance floor, their absence of direction saying they are alone. Their faces say it too, less obviously. But they are not unattractive. The girls look like Pepsi swingers slightly jaded by all the convertibles and the boys are rakish, slim, worldly. And everyone moves with such unconscious surety, such dancer's grace—no, they are not unattractive. But they are alone.

About those who dance: their hair does not blow in the wind; that is Sinclair's vision. It does fly, however, impelled by centrifugal force, and beneath the hair are bodies controlled by an insane puppet master. Grownup bodies which have not yet lost the tree-climbing agility of childhood. Lithe bodies of incredible stamina. Bodies aware of themselves and unashamed.

Sinclair is here and so is his wife, Magdalene, and their year-old baby, Sunny. Magdalene makes amoebae on the walls for a while (it is simply done, with an opaque projector, a dish in which a mixture of oil, water and food coloring is sloshed) and the baby is left with a friend. Later, the baby returned, Magdalene stands watching The Who from close range. Sunny, however, is not impressed; in the midst of all that light and sound and motion, that stunning assault on the senses, she falls asleep.

After a while the environment takes you over and ceases to be something outside your body. You no longer listen to the music or even hear it; it massages you, shakes you, interrupts your thinking and finally dictates, seemingly, the rhythm of your heartbeat. Your eyes accept the flashing lights as normal. It is only when the music and lights go off that your body *starts,* feeling as though lightning has struck, and you become dazed, disoriented.

That time comes, incredibly, and then all the lost children go home to their equally lost parents. No one talks as he leaves the Grande. There is nothing to say. The service is over, the confusing, frustrating, unsatisfying other life they lead is waiting implacably, and as yet there is no permanent alternative.

Soon, though, their faces say. And if Sinclair did not cause their alienation, they have nonetheless picked him as a sort of ideal. Do 16-year-olds "have a good time" making love? They didn't when you were that age, but maybe things have changed since then. The heavens don't split open and they don't lose their teeth, but they do still get pregnant and trapped into decisions they simply can't make, you think.

But Sinclair didn't go out and recruit the kids; they came to him because they didn't believe what their parents were saying anymore. "Now you're starting to get the reaction of kids who were brought up on television," John explains, "who were given a television set to watch when they were born. Who got their education from television. Who have found out from watching television just how vapid and insipid the quote American Way of Life really is.

"You have to realize that television is THE educational medium in the country. The schools now just back up what television teaches you. And what it teaches you is primarily the American Way of Life: white, middle-class, Ozzie and Harriet, McHale's Navy . . . and that whole way of life, you see, has gotten so. far away from what human beings are about—instead it's gotten off into fantasy.

"Like every woman is supposed to wear a girdle and brassiere, all men are supposed to wear suits and ties and have, you know, spray deodorant and boxer shorts, and these are the things that make you a man or a woman."

There is a great deal of play-acting about the hippie world, a large measure of childishness. Laughter comes too easily, before the joke is finished, because there is only one punch line and everybody knows it. The talk is often pointlessly vulgar. The first few times you talk with Sinclair or any of them you are refreshed and stimulated by their charming indifference to all the strait jackets of modern life. After several conversations you begin to understand that, like everyone else, they have only so much to say that is new; having said it they are doomed to repeat themselves again and again. But to them it is new each time.

If there is play-acting and childishness, there is also wisdom and a gentle sweetness that are accentuated by their rarity in the rest of society. And the hippies, whether they are dying out or not, at least demonstrated what never should have required demonstration but somehow did, that it is possible to live in something other than buttondown shirts and neatly trimmed hair.

"The hippies," says Art Johnston, "are trying to develop a code and a life style which are rational for a society of abundance. In all previous societies, survival has been the primary concern, having enough to eat and everything. Now all of a sudden in America we're finding out that we can produce enough for everybody, frequently with less effort.

"And the hippies—most of them are from middle-class families, by the way—they say, 'Well what's the use of being so concerned about money and everything?'

"I think what they're saying is true. In the society of the future we can't be satisfied merely to, you know, work for material rewards."

---

**What Do You Think?**

1.  The title of this article refers to John Sinclair as a "Hippie Evangelist." In what ways is the hippie movement similar to a religion? How does it differ from religious movements?

2.  Some people have suggested that religion-like movements tend to be attractive to people who are alienated. Can you think of any reasons why this might or might not be true? Explain.

## 4.   THE PROBLEM THAT HAS NO NAME *

*The next selection is about the role in our society of the wife and mother. As you read, see if you can identify the main characteristics of "The Problem That Has No Name."*

The problem lay buried, unspoken, for many years in the minds of American women. It was a strange stirring, a sense of dissatisfaction, a yearning that women suffered in the middle of the twentieth century in the United States. Each suburban wife struggled with it alone. As she made beds, shopped for groceries, matched slipcover material, ate peanut butter sandwiches with her children, chauffeured Cub Scouts and Brownies, lay beside her husband at night—she was afraid to ask even of herself the silent question—"Is this all?"

\*     \*     \*     \*     \*

---

* Excerpted from Betty Friedan, *The Feminine Mystique,* New York, N. Y.: W. W. Norton & Company, 1963. By permission of W. W. Norton & Company, Inc. Copyright © 1963 by Betty Friedan.

The suburban housewife—she was the dream image of the young American women and the envy, it was said, of women all over the world. The American housewife—freed by science and labor-saving appliances from the drudgery, the dangers of child-birth and the illnesses of her grandmother. She was healthy, beautiful, educated, concerned only about her husband, her children, her home. She had found true feminine fulfillment. As a housewife and mother, she was respected as a full and equal partner to man in his world. She was free to choose automobiles, clothes, appliances, supermarkets; she had everything that women ever dreamed of. . . .

If a woman had a problem in the 1950's and 1960's, she knew that something must be wrong with her marriage, or with herself. Other women were satisfied with their lives, she thought. What kind of a woman was she if she did not feel this mysterious fulfillment waxing the kitchen floor? She was so ashamed to admit her dissatisfaction that she never knew how many other women shared it. . . .

But on an April morning in 1959, I heard a mother of four, having coffee with four other mothers in a suburban development fifteen miles from New York, say in a tone of quiet desperation, "the problem." And the others knew, without words, that she was not talking about a problem with her husband, or her children, or her home. Suddenly they realized they all shared the same problem, the problem that has no name. They began, hesitantly, to talk about it. Later, after they had picked up their children at nursery school and taken them home to nap, two of the women cried, in sheer relief, just to know they were not alone. . . .

Just what was this problem that has no name? What were the words women used when they tried to express it? Sometimes a woman would say "I feel empty somehow . . . incomplete." Or she would say, "I feel as if I don't exist." Sometimes she blotted out the feeling with a tranquilizer. Sometimes she thought the problem was with her husband, or her children, or that what she really needed was to redecorate her house, or move to a better neighborhood, or have an affair, or another baby. Sometimes, she went to a doctor with symptoms she could hardly describe: "A tired feeling . . . I get so angry with the children it scares me . . . I feel like crying without any reason." . . .

Sometimes a woman would tell me that the feeling gets so strong she runs out of the house and walks through the streets. Or she stays inside her house and cries. Or her children tell her a joke, and she doesn't laugh because she doesn't hear it. I talked to women who had spent years on the analyst's couch, working out their "adjustment to the feminine role," their blocks to "fulfillment as a wife and mother." But the desperate tone in these women's voices, and the look in their eyes, was the same as the tone and the look of other women, who were sure they had no problem, even though they did have a strange feeling of desperation.

A mother of four who left college at nineteen to get married told me:

I've tried everything women are supposed to do—hobbies, gardening, pickling, canning, being very social with my neighbors, joining committees, running PTA teas. I can do it all, and I like it, but it doesn't leave you anything to think about—any feeling of who you are. I never had any career ambitions. All I wanted was to get married and have four children. I love the kids and Bob and my home. There's no problem you can even put a name to. But I'm desperate. I begin to feel I have no personality. I'm a server of food and a putter-on of pants and a bedmaker, somebody who can be called on when you want something. But who am I? . . .

A young wife in a Long Island development said:

I seem to sleep so much. I don't know why I should be so tired. This house isn't nearly so hard to clean as the coldwater flat we had when I was working. The children are at school all day. It's not the work. I just don't feel alive.

\*     \*     \*     \*     \*

Are the women who finished college, the women who once had dreams beyond housewifery, the ones who suffer the most? According to the experts they are, but listen to these four women:

My days are all busy, and dull, too. All I ever do is mess around. I get up at eight—I make breakfast, so I do the dishes, have lunch, do some more dishes and some laundry and cleaning in the afternoon. Then it's supper dishes and I get to sit down a few minutes before the children have to be sent to bed. . . . That's all there is to my day. It's just like any other wife's day. Humdrum. The biggest time, I am chasing kids.

Ye Gods, what do I do with my time? Well, I get up at six. I get my son dressed and then give him breakfast. After that I wash dishes and bathe and feed the baby. Then I get lunch and while the children nap, I sew or mend or iron and do all the other things I can't get done before noon. Then I cook supper for the family and my husband watches TV while I do the dishes. After I get the children to bed, I set my hair and then I go to bed.

The problem is always being the children's mommy, or the minister's wife and never being myself.

A film made of any typical morning in my house would look like an old Marx Brothers' comedy. I wash the dishes, rush the older children off to school, dash out in the yard to cultivate the chrysanthemums, run back in to make a phone call about a committee meeting, help the youngest child build a blockhouse, spend fifteen minutes skimming the newspapers so I can be well-informed, then scamper down to the washing machines where my thrice-weekly laundry includes enough clothes to keep a primitive village going for an entire year. By noon I'm ready for a padded cell. Very little of what I've done has been really necessary or important. Outside pressures lash me through the day. Yet I look upon myself as one of the more relaxed housewives in the neighborhood. Many of my friends are even more frantic. In the past sixty years we have come full circle and the American housewife is once again trapped in a squirrel cage. If the cage is now a modern plate-glass-and-broadloom ranch house or a convenient modern apartment, the situation is no less painful than when her grandmother sat over an embroidery hoop in her gilt-and-plush parlor and muttered angrily about women's rights.

The first two women never went to college. They live in developments in Levittown, New Jersey, and Tacoma, Washington, and were interviewed by a team of sociologists studying workingmen's wives. The third, a minister's wife, wrote on the fifteenth reunion questionnaire of her college that she never had any career ambitions, but wishes now she had. The fourth, who has a Ph.D. in anthropology, is today a Nebraska housewife with three children. Their words seem to indicate that housewives of all educational levels suffer the same feeling of desperation.

---

**What Do You Think?**

1. Some people would say that the problem is that the women described in this reading just don't know when they're well-off. How would you respond to that assertion?

2. If you believe that, in some sense, the assertion above is accurate, would you be willing to characterize those women as being alienated? Why? Why not? Be sure to give reasons for your answer. If you, however, reject the assertion, how would you characterize the sort of attitudes described?

3. Might a man also ask himself the question "Is this all?" Explain.

## 5.   WASTELAND *

*The following short essay by Marya Mannes carries a double-barreled illustration of alienation. As you read it, focus first on Miss Mannes' feelings as she expresses them. Then look back over it—or re-read it —from the perspective that focuses on the conditions about which she is writing.*

Cans. Beer cans. Glinting on the verges of a million miles of roadways, lying in scrub, grass, dirt, leaves, sand, mud, but never hidden. Piel's, Rheingold, Ballantine, Schaefer, Schlitz, shining in the sun or picked by moon or the beams of headlights at night; washed by rain or flattened by wheels, but never dulled, never buried, never destroyed. Here is the mark of savages, the testament of wasters, the stain of prosperity.

Who are these men who defile the grassy borders of our roads and lanes, who pollute our ponds, who spoil the purity of our ocean beaches with the empty vessels of their thirst? Who are the men who make these vessels in millions and then say, "Drink—and discard"? What society is this that can afford to cast away a million tons of metal and to make of wild and fruitful land a garbage heap?

What manner of men and women need thirty feet of steel and two hundred horsepower to take them, singly, to their small destinations? Who demand that what they eat is wrapped so that forests are cut down to make the paper that is thrown away, and what they smoke and chew is sealed so that the sealers can be tossed in gutters and caught in twigs and grass?

What kind of men can afford to make the streets of their towns and cities hideous with neon at night, and their roadways hideous with signs by day, wasting beauty; who leave the carcasses of cars to rot in heaps; who spill their trash into ravines and make smoking mountains of refuse for the town's rats? What manner of men choke off the life in rivers, streams and lakes with the waste of their produce, making poison of water?

Who is as rich as that? Slowly the wasters and despoilers are impoverishing our land, our nature, and our beauty, so that there will not be one beach, one hill, one lane, one meadow, one forest free from the debris of man and the stigma of his improvidence.

Who is so rich that he can squander forever the wealth of earth

---

and water for the trivial needs of vanity or the compulsive demands of greed; or so prosperous in land that he can sacrifice nature for unnatural desires? The earth we abuse and the living things we kill will, in the end, take their revenge; for in exploiting their presence we are diminishing our future.

And what will we leave behind us when we are long dead? Temples? Amphora? Sunken treasure?

Or mountains of twisted, rusted steel, canyons of plastic containers, and a million miles of shores garlanded, not with the lovely wrack of the sea, but with the cans and bottles and light-bulbs and boxes of a people who conserved their convenience at the expense of their heritage, and whose ephemeral prosperity was built on waste.

---

**What Do You Think?**

1. What differences do you see between Miss Mannes' alienation and that of the people about whom she wrote?
2. Compare this selection with "Thirty-eight Witnesses"—the third selection in the opening chapter. What similarities and differences do you find?
3. How do *you* feel about Miss Mannes' essay? Why?

## 6. THE POLITE FICTION *

*The next selection describes a paradoxical sequence of events that took place in the offices of a factory. As you read it, try to relate the episodes with the characteristics of alienation that you read about in Chapter 2.*

One afternoon, a conversation with the manager led to his talking about the effects of promotion on different men in the factory, and, eventually, to something of a diatribe against one particular person who had moved up into an executive position the year before. He had tried to get support for the promotion from everybody, he had blackened the man who was leaving and whose position he hoped to fill, had gone into local politics on the same side as the divisional manager, had displayed unpleasant anxiety when the time came for the decision. Now, despite his fulsome affability, he was unpopular with his colleagues, was looked on by those lower down as a tale-bearer, and so on. All this was delivered

---

* Excerpted from Tom Burns, "Friends, Enemies, and the Polite Fiction," *American Sociological Review,* December 1953.

with gestures and emphasis distinctly more lively than earlier in the conversation, which ended with this episode, both of us returning to separate desks.

Later in the afternoon, he telephoned the man of whom he had been speaking; there was question of the allocation of a morning's time put in by a shiftworker in one or the other of their departments. The whole matter of dispute was handled with the greatest mateyness and ease; first names were used, there was no sense of effort in maintaining the demonstration of friendliness; there was no over-emphasis, nor, on the other hand, any discrepancy between facial expression and words or tone of voice; each other's account of the facts was fully accepted and agreement quickly reached.

Inside the space of one hour, my companion had displayed quite marked enmity and equally well-marked friendship toward the same person. There was, as far as I judge, no suspicion of awareness that there was any incompatibility between the two episodes—both were acted through natural expression of two distinct roles.

---

**What Do You Think?**

1.  Some people would describe the manager's behavior as hypocritical. Would you accept that description? Why? Why not?
2.  What causes an individual to behave like this?
3.  Do you believe that it would be better for the manager to let his associate know how he feels about him? Why? Why not? How *does* the manager feel about his associate?

## 7.  THE EXURBANITE AT WORK *

*Most of us are familiar with the "suburbanite"—the man who lives in one of the suburbs that surround our larger cities, but whose work takes him daily into the city itself. Probably fewer of us, however, are familiar with the "exurbanite." The writer of the following selection coined that term to refer to the man who, though still working in the city, has "escaped" from the suburbs to the "exurbs" beyond. Though it is his greater affluence that made possible the exurbanite's flight from suburbia, the writer's view of the exurbanite at work, as you will see, is not one of smooth sailing in calm seas.*

---

. . . An exurbanite . . . is the managing editor of a national monthly magazine, a position, it would be assumed, that would insure a certain security. And so it did, until he moved out of town. The trouble is, his boss, the editor-in-chief, is still fanatically urban. The magazine's hours have always been nine-thirty to five-thirty, its tempo has always been relatively relaxed, rarely has there been need for anyone to work later than six, except for a few days a month, just before closing deadlines. The managing editor could with ease catch a six o'clock train to his exurb and did, for the first few weeks. Then his attention was arrested by an apparently idle, aimless remark his editor underhanded him.

"Oh, by the way, Bob," said this editor, "a few of us were sitting around the office last night, talking about the front of the book. You know, some of the young guys around here have a lot of good ideas about how to fix it up."

"Why didn't you call me in?"

"We looked for you, but you'd gone. Don't worry about it, Bob, I can give you all that was said in a memo. That'll cover it."

"Gosh, Joe, if you're thinking of having any more of these editorial meetings, I'd like to know about them. I can always plan to stay late, you know. . . ."

"Sure, sure, forget it. This was just one of those impromptu bull sessions. Valuable, when they, you know, get the spark that some of these youngsters seem to have. I'll send you a memo."

Since then this managing editor has been staying around the office, staring at articles in his slush pile, until he is sure his editor has gone home. Both used to leave by six at the latest. Sometimes, now, the managing editor misses even the 7:08.

\*      \*      \*      \*      \*

There was once . . . an agency that boasted the names of three partners on its letterhead. This story concerns the two men whose names came first. The senior of these two, the senior partner of the firm, was, despite his exalted position [anxiety-ridden], and he had reason, for his junior was an adept at a form of attrition which might be called name-dropping in reverse. Junior was skilled at seeming to know a great deal, perhaps everything, of what went on even on Senior's accounts. He had pipe lines. He never mentioned names. Sometimes he never even spoke. But his expression was eloquent. His expression said: "I've been talking to the sales manager, over at the client's office. I hope things aren't as bad as he seemed to think they were." And Senior squirmed.

Senior's principal client was a very large and important client indeed, with offices in Cleveland. Regularly Senior would take a plane to Cleveland, sometimes just for wetnursing, sometimes on important business.

Once he went to deliver a big presentation. Much headway was made; the contract seemed assured, for increased billing. While he was on his way back, Junior put in a phone call to Cleveland, and did no more than say hello to a friend at the client's office. Presently Senior walked in, and Junior looked at him, his face wearing that inscrutable expression that seemed to suggest so much. Senior, who had arrived exultant, almost singing, felt his stomach turn over. Did Junior know something?

"Hi," said Junior. "I was just talking to Cleveland. Things don't seem so bad—" tiny pause "—after all."

That was all he said, and it should be pointed out that Junior and Senior were good friends, and that actually Junior had no wish to go poking around in Senior's business. But he couldn't help himself. He had always acted that way, and he always will. For him to say such a thing, for him to add fuel to the fire of Senior's fear as to whether the account was shaky, was not in the nature of a ploy in a game of one-upmanship; it was the way of his life. Had Junior deliberately intended that it should end as it did? We will never know; but today there are only two names on the agency's letterhead, and Junior's is senior.

\*     \*     \*     \*     \*

A caveat belongs here. The reader unfamiliar with this working milieu must not think that all the jockeying for position is a matter of conscious conniving. Ask the average communications man if he's guilty of it and he'll be hurt. Of course not. It doesn't apply in his case. He works hard, is simple and straightforward, is filled with esteem and regard for his fellows and wants nothing but the best for them. He's aware, of course, that bitchery, back stabbing, and assassination by innuendo are prevalent in his business, but he himself is innocent and so are the people with whom he works. "It's true," he'll insist. "In our outfit there's temperament, of course, but conscious throat cutting? No."

The operative word is "conscious." It isn't always consciously intended, but the throat cutting goes on, throughout the communications world.

\*     \*     \*     \*     \*

The president of a large and important public relations firm has under him four vice-presidents. They have all been in their jobs for pleasantly lengthy periods, anywhere from seven to fifteen years; they are all well paid. But they are all unnerved: when the president goes with one of them to lunch, the other three worry. "What's going on? What's he telling him? What's going to happen?" And down through the chain of command, each vice-president thereafter, in a formal pecking order, endeavors to do the same to his underlings, and they to theirs.

One of these vice-presidents is a commuter. To try to compensate for the exposed position his train schedule leaves him in every evening, he resorts to elaborate expedients. For example, it had been his custom while he lived in the city to patronize a barbershop near his home, a small but good one where the same man had been ministering to him, in the manner he had taught him, for many years. Recently, however, he learned that his boss (as well as other important contacts) patronized the barbershop of an East Fifties hotel. It took quite some conniving to get on the regular, by-appointment, client list there, but the v.p. figured it was worth it. The day he was admitted to the club, when he could tell his secretary to call and make an appointment for him (having learned this was the boss's day, too) he felt he'd pulled off a major coup. He felt so good about it, in fact, that he wandered down the hall and beamingly reported the fact to a colleague, straight-faced and unashamed. The colleague, with typical communications-business, bitchy crackmanship said, "Bully for you; maybe some day I can get you into the men's room at the Ritz." The vice-president was quick to laugh—at himself and with the other man—but only after a lightning estimate, casing the situation (What goes on in that men's room? Really worth going to? Get biz? Meet the right people?) and then instantly rejecting the notion as absurd.

---

**What Do You Think?**

1. Imagine that you are one of the persons described in one of the previous episodes. How would you feel about your work?
2. Why might an individual "stay with" a job of the sort described in these episodes?

## 8. THE MAN ON THE ASSEMBLY LINE *

*Having had a "view from the top," shift your perspective to that of the "little guy"—the worker in the factory. This reading reports the results of a study of the attitudes of the workers in one plant of a large manufacturing concern. How do their attitudes compare with those expressed in the prior two readings?*

In the undirected part of our preliminary interviews it was found that nearly every worker expressed an opinion about the company and almost always in terms of what Plant X or Company X was doing for him or for some other employee, whether much or little. Accordingly, we framed a

* Excerpted from C. R. Walker and R. H. Guest, *The Man on the Assembly Line,* Cambridge, Mass.: Harvard University Press, Copyright 1952, by the President and Fellows of Harvard College.

question as follows: "Do you think the company (1) does all it can for the men? (2) does something, but not all it could do? (3) doesn't do much of anything?"

    (1)   . . . 11.1 per cent . . . of the . . . men who were interviewed said that the company did all it could for the men.

    (2)   . . . 36.1 per cent . . . said that the company did something for the men but not all it could.

    (3)   . . . 52.2 per cent . . . said that the company did not do much of anything for the men.

\*    \*    \*    \*    \*

These very general summaries of attitudes become more meaningful when we turn to the qualitative comments which workers gave in explanation of them.

Typical of those who thought "the company does all it can for the men" were such comments as:

The company has really helped a lot. They have brought security to a great many men who never had it before.

They're pretty good with the men—lavoratories, bathrooms, showers, and a good hospital.

The company looked out for me first rate. I cut my hand. They took care of me and gave me a light job. They used me very well.

Under the existing conditions I would say the company was doing everything possible for the men. After all, they are running a business. It's the work that's rough, but it's a good outfit.

Turn now to the second group, those who said the company "does something, but not all it could do." This group might be called the mixed favorable and unfavorable group. The positive side of their comments covered a variety of factors such as high pay, job security, good working conditions, and so forth. On the negative side, a majority of comments were tied to two themes: (1) disliked characteristics of the assembly line, for which the company as a rule was blamed; (2) alleged company disregard of the individual. Some combined a favorable attitude to the company with an unfavorable one toward the assembly line:

Sometimes the company does what it can, sometimes not. Departments are different. Some departments realize the men are human and that the line is no fun.

The company has done a lot for me. They asked for blood donors on the bulletin board and they saved my daughter's life—and saved me paying for the blood. But the work itself is a steady grind.

The only thing bothering everybody is the speed. They ought to slow down or hire more men.

They could do more to improve conditions, and it would pay them. For instance, they could give scheduled breaks during the day.

I like the medical service they give. Also, the job gives me better living conditions; that's the main thing. But the monotony of the job and the speed of the line are bad. It doesn't bother me so much now, but it will in ten years. I'd rather work for less at less speed.

Below are remarks of those whose unfavorable comments concerned the company's disregard of the individual:

It's a big outfit; they're strict. They can't deal with an individual. They can only consider groups.

The company tries to do some things, but it wants to get the cars out. They are first, and the men are second.

As far as hospital treatment goes, the company goes all the way. But they treat the men like one of the machines.

The company tries to please everybody, but it is impossible to please a huge group.

The company gives the men a good break often. It doesn't do everything, but it does more than many large companies.

We turn now to the comments of the third group, those who said the company "doesn't do much of anything" for the men. A similar pattern of criticism emerges here, but in phrases carrying more emotional impact. As before, the majority of unfavorable comments were concerned either with the workers' dislike for assembly line work or with the company's alleged disregard of the individual. Typical comments of those who disliked the line were the following:

The men on the line have too much work for the time allowed. The company just cares for production, not the men at all.

The company is against the worker. It changes the lunch hour or cuts it off so that a line can catch up. The line goes so fast that guys can't keep up, especially new guys. This results in inferior work, so the company gets behind. Overtime and short lunch hours result.

The worst is the pressure. It's like on a dog-sled. As soon as the whistle blows, they yell "Mush," and away you go producing cars. The company should at least give us a five-minute break. Or the pace could be slower. The only good thing the company has is a hospital, and that is really good.

That group of workers who were generally unfavorable to the company but who criticized it in more general terms for what appeared to them a disregard of themselves as individuals commented as follows:

I'm left with the impression that the company doesn't think so much of the individual. If it did, they wouldn't have a production line like this one.

The place is run like the Army. They should think more about the men than the product they put out. They could do a lot more.

You're just a number to them. They number the stock, and they number you. . . .

As long as they get the cars out, they don't give a damn for the man.

It's a big concern. They are out to make money, and they don't care how they do it. They don't care how the men feel; they only care about money. If I were in their position, I'd probably be that way too, but they ignore the way the men feel.

The company just thinks of the men as robots. If they get the cars out, they don't care what happens to the men. The bigger the company, the less they do for the men. The engineers never talk to us except on business.

---

**What Do You Think?**

> What similarities do you see between the attitudes expressed or implied in this reading and those in the two prior readings? What differences do you see? Refer to specific statements to support your views.

## ↗ 9.   THE ALIENATED CONSUMER *

> *If alienation is found at many levels in the businesses and manufacturing concerns of this country, what about the people who purchase the goods and services these businesses produce? In the next selection the writer deals with that question.*

The process of *consumption* is as alienated as the process of production. In the first place, we acquire things with money; we are accustomed

---

* Excerpted from Erich Fromm, *The Sane Society,* New York, N. Y.: Holt, Rinehart and Winston, 1955. Copyright © 1955 by Erich Fromm. Reprinted by permission of Holt, Rinehart and Winston, Inc.

to this and take it for granted. But actually, this is a most peculiar way of acquiring things. Money represents labor and effort in an abstract form; not necessarily *my* labor and *my* effort, since I can have acquired it by inheritance, by fraud, by luck, or any number of ways. But even if I have acquired it by *my* effort . . . , I have acquired it in a specific way, by a specific kind of effort, corresponding to my skills and capacities, while, in spending, the money is transformed into an abstract form of labor and can be exchanged against anything else. Provided I am in the possession of money, no effort or interest of mine is necessary to acquire something. If I have the money, I can acquire an exquisite painting, even though I may not have any appreciation for art; I can buy the best phonograph, even though I have no musical taste; I can buy a library, although I use it only for the purpose of ostentation. I can buy an education, even though I have no use for it except as an additional social asset. I can even destroy the painting or the books I bought, and aside from a loss of money, I suffer no damage.

\*     \*     \*     \*     \*

But beyond the method of acquisition, how do we use things, once we have acquired them? With regard to many things, there is not even the pretense of use. We acquire them to *have* them. We are satisfied with useless possession. The expensive dining set or crystal vase which we never use for fear they might break, the mansion with many unused rooms, the unnecessary cars and servants, like ugly bric-a-brac of the lower-middle-class family, are so many examples of pleasure in possession instead of in use. However, this satisfaction in possessing per se was more prominent in the nineteenth century; today most of the satisfaction is derived from possession of things-to-be-used rather than of things-to-be-kept. This does not alter the fact, however, that even in the pleasure of things-to-be-used the satisfaction of prestige is a paramount factor. The car, the refrigerator, the television set are for real, but also for conspicuous use. They confer status on the owner.

\*     \*     \*     \*     \*

There is another aspect of alienation from the things we consume which needs to be mentioned. We are surrounded by things of whose nature and origin we know nothing. The telephone, radio, phonograph, and all other complicated machines are almost as mysterious to us as they would be to a man from a primitive culture; we know how to use them, that is, we know which button to turn, but we do not know on what principle they function, except in the vaguest terms of something we once learned at school. And things which do not rest upon difficult scientific principles are almost equally alien to us. We do not know how bread is made, how cloth is woven, how a table is manufactured, how glass is made. We consume, as we produce, without any concrete relatedness to the objects with which we deal; we live in a world of things, and our only connection with them is that we know how to manipulate or to consume them.

\*     \*     \*     \*     \*

The alienated attitude toward consumption not only exists in our acquisition and consumption of commodities, but it determines far beyond this the employment of leisure time. . . .

In any productive and spontaneous activity, something happens within myself while I am reading, looking at scenery, talking to friends, etcetera. I am not the same after the experience as I was before. In the alienated form of pleasure nothing happens within me; I have consumed this or that; nothing is changed within myself, and all that is left are memories of what I have done. One of the most striking examples for this kind of pleasure consumption is the taking of snapshots, which has become one of the most significant leisure activities. The Kodak slogan, "You press the button, we do the rest," which since 1889 has helped so much to popularize photography all over the world, is symbolic. It is one of the earliest appeals to push-button power-feeling; you do nothing, you do not have to know anything, everything is done for you; all you have to do is to press the button. Indeed, the taking of snapshots has become one of the most significant expressions of alienated visual perception, of sheer consumption. The "tourist" with his camera is an outstanding symbol of an alienated relationship to the world. Being constantly occupied with taking pictures, actually *he* does not see anything at all, except through the intermediary of the camera. The camera sees for him, and the outcome of his "pleasure" trip is a collection of snapshots, which are the substitute for an experience which he could have had, but did not have.

---

**What Do You Think?**

>  According to the author, our alienation from the things we acquire is related to the method of acquisition, our use of the things once we have them, and our knowledge of those things. Can you think of some common everyday examples that illustrate the author's point? Can you think of some instances that could be viewed as exceptions to his point?

## 10.  THE INVISIBLE MAN *

*The problem of the relationship of black Americans to American society has been viewed historically, educationally, politically, economically, and demographically—to mention but a few perspectives—in recent years. In the next selection you will have an opportunity to explore something of what it feels like to be black in our country.*

I am an invisible man. No, I am not a spook like those who haunted Edgar Allan Poe. . . . I am a man of substance, of flesh and bone, fiber and liquids—and I might even be said to possess a mind. I am invisible, understand, simply because people refuse to see me. . . . When they approach me they see only my surroundings, themselves, or figments of their imagination—indeed, everything and anything except me. . . .

That invisibility to which I refer occurs because of a peculiar disposition of the eyes of those with whom I come in contact. A matter of the construction of their *inner* eyes, those eyes with which they look through their physical eyes upon reality. . . . You're constantly being bumped against by those of poor vision. Or again, you often doubt if you really exist. You wonder whether you aren't simply a phantom in other people's minds. . . . It's when you feel like this that, out of resentment, you begin to bump people back. And, let me confess, you feel that way most of the time. You ache with the need to convince yourself that you do exist in the real world, that you're a part of all the sound and anguish, and you strike out with your fists, you curse and you swear to make them recognize you. And, alas, it's seldom successful.

One night I accidentally bumped into a man, and perhaps because of the near darkness he saw me and called me an insulting name. I sprang at him, seized his coat lapels and demanded that he apologize. He was a tall blond man, and as my face came close to his he looked insolently out of his blue eyes and cursed me, his breath hot in my face as he struggled. I pulled his chin down sharp upon the crown of my head, butting him as I had seen the West Indians do, and I felt his flesh tear and the blood gush out, and I yelled, "Apologize. Apologize!" But he continued to curse and struggle, and I butted him again and again until he went down heavily, on his knees, profusely bleeding. I kicked him repeatedly, in a frenzy because he still uttered insults though his lips were frothy with blood. Oh yes, I kicked him! And in my outrage I got

---

* Excerpted from Ralph Ellison, *Invisible Man,* New York, N. Y.: Random House, Inc. Copyright 1952 by Ralph Ellison. Reprinted by permission of Random House, Inc.

out my knife and prepared to slit his throat, right there beneath the lamplight in the deserted street, holding him by the collar with one hand, and opening the knife with my teeth—when it occurred to me that the man had not *seen* me, actually; that he, as far as he knew, was in the midst of a walking nightmare! And I stopped the blade, slicing the air as I pushed him away, letting him fall back to the street. I stared at him hard as the lights of a car stabbed through the darkness. He lay there, moaning on the asphalt; a man almost killed by a phantom. It unnerved me. I was both disgusted and ashamed. I was like a drunken man myself, wavering about on weakened legs. Then I was amused. Something in this man's thick head had sprung out and beaten him within an inch of his life. I began to laugh at this crazy discovery. Would he have awakened at the point of death? Would Death himself have freed him for wakeful living? But I didn't linger. I ran away into the dark, laughing so hard I feared I might rupture myself. The next day I saw his picture in the *Daily News,* beneath a caption stating that he had been "mugged." Poor fool, poor blind fool, I thought with sincere compassion, mugged by an invisible man!

---

**What Do You Think?**

1.    Which of the characteristics of alienation that were discussed in Chapter 2 do you find manifested in this excerpt?
2.    How would you describe the feelings expressed by the writer?

## 11.    THE MEANING OF A "CONK" *

*The reading on the previous pages was written by a prominent black American author in a novel published in 1952; the next selection was taken from the autobiography of a leading black revolutionary shortly before he was assassinated in 1964. As you read, compare the feelings expressed by the two men in these selections.*

When Shorty let me stand up and see in the mirror, my hair hung down in limp, damp strings. My scalp still flamed, but not as badly; I could bear it. He draped the towel around my shoulders, over my rubber apron, and began again vaselining my hair.

I could feel him combing, straight back, first the big comb, then the fine-tooth one.

---

* Excerpted from *The Autobiography of Malcolm X.* Reprinted by permission of Grove Press, Inc. Copyright © 1964 by Alex Haley and Malcolm X. Copyright © 1965 by Alex Haley and Betty Shabazz.

Then, he was using a razor, very delicately, on the back of my neck. Then, finally, shaping the sideburns.

My first view in the mirror blotted out the hurting. I'd seen some pretty conks, but when it's the first time, on your *own* head, the transformation, after the lifetime of kinks, is staggering.

The mirror reflected Shorty behind me. We both were grinning and sweating. And on top of my head was this thick, smooth sheen of shining red hair—real red—as straight as any white man's.

How ridiculous I was! Stupid enough to stand there simply lost in admiration of my hair now looking "white," reflected in the mirror in Shorty's room. I vowed that I'd never again be without a conk, and I never was for many years.

This was my first really big step toward self-degradation: when I endured all of that pain, literally burning my flesh to have it look like a white man's hair. I had joined the multitude of Negro men and women in America who are brainwashed into believing that the black people are "inferior"—and white people "superior"—that they will even violate and mutilate their God-created bodies to try to look "pretty" by white standards.

Look around today, in every small town and big city, from two-bit catfish and soda-pop joints into the "integrated" lobby of the Waldorf-Astoria, and you'll see conks on black men. And you'll see black women wearing these green and pink and purple and red and platinum-blonde wigs. They're all more ridiculous than a slapstick comedy. It makes you wonder if the Negro has completely lost his sense of identity, lost touch with himself.

You'll see the conk worn by many, many so-called "upper class" Negroes, and, as much as I hate to say it about them, on all too many Negro entertainers. One of the reasons that I've especially admired some of them, like Lionel Hampton and Sidney Poitier, among others, is that they have kept their natural hair and fought to the top. I admire any Negro man who has never had himself conked, or who has had the sense to get rid of it—as I finally did.

I don't know which kind of self-defacing conk is the greater shame—the one you'll see on the heads of the black so-called "middle class" and "upper class," who ought to know better, or the one you'll see on the heads of the poorest, most downtrodden, ignorant black men. I mean the legal-minimum-wage ghetto-dwelling kind of Negro, as I was when I got my first one. It's generally among these poor fools that you'll see a black kerchief over the man's head, like Aunt Jemima; he's trying to make his conk last longer, between trips to the barbershop. Only for special occasions is this kerchief-protected conk exposed—to show off how "sharp" and "hip" its owner is. The ironic thing is that I have never heard any woman, white or black, express any admiration for a conk. Of course, any white woman with a black man isn't thinking about his hair. But I don't see how on earth a black woman with any race pride could walk down the street with any black man wearing a conk—the emblem of his shame that he is black.

---

**What Do You Think?**

1.   The attempt by some black Americans to adopt the styles of white society is viewed by Malcolm X as a manifestation of alienation. Would the same be true of the adoption by many white young people of music and dance steps developed in the black community? Why or why not?

2.   In this selection Malcolm X refers to the widespread use of conks by black men. Since Malcolm X's death, black men (and women, too) have turned in increasing numbers to the "natural" hair style, and the conk is seen less and less frequently. What inference would you draw from this fact regarding the black American's alienation?

## 12.   FIFTH AVENUE, UPTOWN *

*The final selection on the problem of alienation in the black community shifts the focus from the individual to a broader view of life in the big city ghetto.*

The avenue is elsewhere the renowned and elegant Fifth. The area I am describing, which, in today's gang parlance, would be called "the turf," is bounded by Lenox Avenue on the west, the Harlem River on the east, 135th Street on the north, and 130th Street on the south. We never lived beyond these boundaries; this is where we grew up. . . . When I turn east on 131st Street and Lenox Avenue, there is first a soda-pop joint, then a shoeshine "parlor," then a grocery store, then a dry cleaners', then the houses. All along the street there are people who watched me grow up, people who grew up with me, people I watched grow up with my brothers and sisters; and, sometimes in my arms, sometimes underfoot, sometimes at my shoulder—or on it—their children, a riot, a forest of children, who include my nieces and nephews.

When we reach the end of this long block, we find ourselves on wide, filthy, hostile Fifth Avenue, facing that project which hangs over the av-

---

* Reprinted from James Baldwin, *Nobody Knows My Name*. Copyright © 1954, 1956, 1958, 1959, 1960, 1961 by James Baldwin and used by permission of the publisher, The Dial Press, Inc.

enue like a monument to the folly, and the cowardice, of good intentions. All along the block, for anyone who knows it, are immense human gaps, like craters. These gaps are not created merely by those who have moved away, inevitably into some other ghetto; or by those who have risen, almost always into a greater capacity for self-loathing and self-delusion; or yet by those who, by whatever means—World War II, the Korean war, a policeman's gun or billy, a gang war, a brawl, madness, an overdose of heroin, or, simply, unnatural exhaustion—are dead. I am talking about those who are left, and I am talking principally about the young. What are they doing? Well, some, a minority, are fanatical churchgoers, members of the more extreme of the Holy Roller sects. Many, many more are "Moslems," by affiliation or sympathy, that is to say that they are united by nothing more—and nothing less—than a hatred of the white world and all its works. They are present, for example, at every Buy Black streetcorner meeting—meetings in which the speaker urges his hearers to cease trading with white men and establish a separate economy. Neither the speaker nor his hearers can possibly do this, of course, since Negroes do not own General Motors or RCA or the A & P, nor, indeed, do they own more than a wholly insufficient fraction of anything else in Harlem (those who *do* own anything are more interested in their profits than in their fellows). But these meetings nevertheless keep alive in the participators a certain pride of bitterness without which, however futile this bitterness may be, they could scarcely remain alive at all. Many have given up. They stay home and watch the TV screen living on the earnings of their parents, cousins, brothers, or uncles, and only leave the house to go to the movies or to the nearest bar. "How're you making it?" one may ask, running into them along the block, or in the bar. "Oh, I'm TV-ing it"; with the saddest, sweetest, most shamefaced of smiles and from a great distance. This distance one is compelled to respect; anyone who has traveled so far will not easily be dragged again into the world. There are further retreats, of course, than the TV screen or the bar. There are those who are simply sitting on their stoops, "stoned," animated for a moment only, and hideously, by the approach of someone who may lend them the money for a "fix." Or by the approach of someone from whom they can purchase it, one of the shrewd ones, on the way to prison or just coming out.

And the others, who have avoided all of these deaths, get up in the morning and go downtown to meet "the man." They work in the white man's world all day and come home in the evening to this fetid block. They struggle to instill in their children some private sense of honor or dignity which will help the child to survive. This means, of course, that they must struggle, stolidly, incessantly, to keep this sense alive in themselves, in spite of the insults, the indifference, and the cruelty they are certain to encounter in their working day. They patiently browbeat the landlord into fixing the heat, the plaster, the plumbing; this demands prodigious patience; nor is patience usually enough. In trying to make their hovels habitable, they are perpetually throwing good money after bad. Such frustration, so long endured, is driving many strong, admirable men and women whose only crime is color to the very gates of paranoia.

\*     \*     \*     \*     \*

It is a terrible, an inexorable, law that one cannot deny the humanity of another without diminishing one's own: in the face of one's victim, one sees oneself. Walk through the streets of Harlem and see what we, this nation, have become.

---

**What Do You Think?**

1.  Baldwin says that "one cannot deny the humanity of another without diminishing one's own." What does he mean? What relevance does that comment have for your study of alienation?
2.  What characteristics of alienation are you able to identify in this selection?
3.  How would you describe the feelings Baldwin expresses through his writing about "Fifth Avenue, Uptown"?

## 13.  THE ALIENATED VOTER *

*This article reports the results of a study of voting behavior and voter attitudes. Ask yourself, as you read, whether the feelings and perceptions reported here are widespread across our nation.*

On November 7, 1960, the voters of Massachusetts, despite their strong affection for John F. Kennedy and their customary allegiance to the Democratic Party, elected John Volpe, a Republican, as Governor of the Commonwealth. Volpe, a relatively unknown underdog, upset Joseph Ward, the Democratic candidate, by 138,485 votes, although Kennedy received a plurality in excess of half a million. Two months before Volpe's victory, Ward, who was the endorsee of the Democratic Party pre-primary convention, defeated six Democratic Party chieftains (one of whom was named John F. Kennedy) who opposed him in the primary. In November 1959 another relatively unknown underdog, John Collins, was elected mayor of Boston when he defeated John Powers, president of the state

* Excerpted from Murray Levin and Murray Eden, "The Alienated Voter," *Public Opinion Quarterly*, 26. Reprinted by permission of the publisher.

senate and one of the most powerful figures in the Democratic Party.

Although these three elections seem to have little in common—they took place at different times, in different constituencies, and involved different offices—they are, in fact, expressions of a common phenomenon, voter cynicism, anger, and alienation. . . .

In each case public opinion studies reveal that between 20 and 50 per cent of the respondents who voted "for" the winner actually voted against the loser, that is, for the candidate perceived as "the lesser of two evils. . . ."

(Unless otherwise indicated, the quotations which appear . . . are taken from public opinion surveys relating to these elections.)

"I don't like the caliber of the candidates." "Of the worst he was the best. All a bunch of chiselers." "Volpe is not quite as bad as Ward. I didn't have anything better to vote for." "Not much to offer between either—almost left it blank." "Felt they were all no good." . . .

Many respondents who voted did so on the assumption that it made no difference which candidate won because both candidates were perceived as selfish or crooked. . . .

"Doesn't matter who wins on the state level, they are all crooks." "Things always turn out the same no matter who wins." "It makes no difference who wins, Massachusetts is just a crappy state. You can't do anything with it. There is something wrong here." "Voting wouldn't do any good—they're both no good." "Well, voting only decides between the politicians." "Once they get into office, that's the end of what we have to say." "They care only to win elections." . . .

The contributors and the candidates in each of these elections form, in the view of many respondents, an oligarchy which controls the community in its own interest. Many respondents also complained that the candidates did not present a serious and meaningful discussion of the issues and that the rhetoric of the campaign had been reduced to mutual character assassination, which made it impossible to tell who was telling the truth. These attitudes reflect the fact that in recent years several investigations into various branches of the state government and the government of Boston have revealed pervasive conflict of interest and outright corruption.

Assuming that politicians are corrupt, these citizens have concluded that voting is useless, reform impossible, and the so-called democratic process a hollow mockery of what it is supposed to be. They structure the political word in terms of a sharp dichotomy between the powerful insiders—politicians, contractors, bookies, big businessmen—and the voters, who are powerless outsiders. . . .

Alienated voters are hostile to politicians and disenchanted with the political process. They are wary of candidates who spend large sums of money during campaigns. They are skeptical of those who are endorsed by powerful "public" figures, and they tend to believe that campaign promises and platforms are empty verbiage. If they vote at all, it is against the "greater evil," against the "politician," against the well-financed, and against the powerful. They do not really vote "for" anyone.

---

**What Do You Think?**

    1.    Do you believe that the feelings and attitudes expressed above are prevalent in this country? What evidence can you cite to support your view?

    2.    Have you ever expressed attitudes similar to those expressed in the article? In what connection? Would you conclude, if your answer was "yes," that in that respect you were alienated? Why? Why not? It might be helpful to refer to the several characteristics of alienation described in Chapter 2.

**ACTIVITIES FOR INVOLVEMENT**

    1.    In the readings in this chapter there are represented a number of different groups of Americans among whom feelings of alienation appear to be particularly prevalent. Identify these groups. Then, using that list, prepare a chart in which you list the characteristics of alienation that these groups possess and the direction toward which their alienation is aimed. Refer again to Chapter 2, if necessary. Be sure that you can support the inferences that you make in the chart with specific references to the appropriate readings in this chapter.

    2.    One way that it is possible for a person to empathize or "feel for" another person is to try to *be* that person for a very brief period. Select several of the situations described in the readings and role-play them along with your classmates. Be sure that you try to portray accurately as well as imaginatively the person whose identity you are assuming. Let several students in the class portray the same role. Have some students who are not directly involved in the role-playing serve as observers and commentators to suggest how the role-playing exercise might be improved. Upon completion of each episode, hold a class discussion in which the students who did the role-playing describe how they felt as they played their roles.

    3.    One might well raise the question as to whether the individuals identified in this chapter really represent a number of people with similar feelings. While the question is too complex for you to answer fully, you could gather some data by preparing and using a questionnaire in which you raise some of the concerns that the individuals in this chapter express. Conduct your interviews among a random sample of friends. What are they most concerned about? What differences do you notice between their concerns and those of the individuals in this chapter? Similarities? How would you explain these differences and similarities? Report your findings to the class for discussion.

4.     Look back over the chart that you made in response to the first question. Prepare a list of possible explanations for the prevalence of alienation in each of those groups. As you read the next chapter, see how many of your explanations "check out" against the readings there. Write an essay in which you attempt to explain any which do not check out.

5.     Organize a debate in your class on the following proposition: "Resolved: That the litterbug is alienated."

6.     Using current editions of newspapers and newsmagazines, make a collection of articles that seem to you to suggest evidence of alienation. Compare your collection with those of your classmates, and then draft a letter to your school or community newspaper in which you suggest how such alienation develops.

7.     A number of different adjectives have been used to describe those individuals who have been classified (by some) as alienated. From the list below, pick the five which you feel are *most* appropriate and the five which are *least* appropriate. Be prepared to defend your choice. Then compare your list with those of your classmates and see if you can form a master list of those words which most accurately describe the alienated individual. Hold a class discussion on how such alienation might be reduced.

| | | |
|---|---|---|
| bored | caring | wondering |
| disaffected | distrusting | involved |
| hurt | irritated | concerned |
| angry | puzzled | warm |
| loving | apathetic | cold |
| torn | distraught | lost |
| mixed-up | sick | affectionate |

# What Are the Alienating Pressures Today?

**4**

In Chapter 3 the focus was on people—we were seeking to identify various groups of Americans who seem to be alienated and to learn something about the meaning of alienation. This chapter presents a broader perspective: it explores various forces and institutions in modern life that appear to be contributing to the widespread alienation in America. As you read the following selections, try to relate the conditions and situations described in them to the feelings and attitudes expressed in Chapter 3.

### 1.   POOR SCHOLAR'S SOLILOQUY *

*In the following selection, the writer attempts to look at schools and education through the eyes of a seventh-grade boy. Does he describe your school experience?*

No, I'm not very good in school. This is my second year in the seventh grade and I'm bigger and taller than the other kids. They like me all right, though, even if I don't say much in the schoolroom, because outside I can tell them how to do lots of things. They tag me around and that sort of makes up for what goes on in school.

I don't know why the teachers don't like me. They never have very much. Seems like they don't think you know anything unless they can

---

* Excerpted from Stephen M. Corey, "The Poor Scholar's Soliloquy," *Childhood Education,* January 1944. Reprinted by permission of Stephen M. Corey and the Association for Childhood Education International, 3615 Wisconsin Avenue, N. W., Washington, D. C. Copyright © 1944 by the Association.

name the book it comes out of. I've got a lot of books in my own room at home—books like *Popular Science, Mechanical Encyclopedia,* and the *Sears'* and *Ward's* catalogues, but I don't very often just sit down and read them through like they make us do in school. I use my books when I want to find something out, like whenever Mom buys anything second-hand I look it up in the Sears' or Ward's first and tell her if she got stung or not. I can use the index in a hurry to find things I want.

In school, though, we've got to learn whatever is in the book and I just can't memorize the stuff. Last year I stayed after school every night for two weeks trying to learn the names of the Presidents. I am taking the seventh grade over but our teacher this year isn't so interested in the names of the Presidents. She has us trying to learn the names of all the great American inventors.

### KIDS SEEMED INTERESTED

I guess I can't remember names in history. Anyway, this year I've been trying to learn about trucks because my uncle owns three and he says I can drive one when I'm sixteen. I already know the horsepower and number of forward and backward speeds of twenty-six American trucks, some of the Diesels, and I can spot each make a long way off. It's funny how that Diesel works. I started to tell my teacher about it last Wednesday in science class when the pump we were using to make a vacuum in a bell jar got hot, but she said she didn't see what a Diesel engine had to do with our experiment on air pressure so I just kept still. The kids seemed interested though. I took four of them around to my uncle's garage after school and we saw the mechanic, Gus, tearing a big truck Diesel down. Boy, does he know his stuff!

I'm not very good in geography either. They call it economic geography this year. We've been studying the imports and exports of Chile all week but I couldn't tell you what they are. Maybe the reason is I had to miss school yesterday because my uncle took me and his big trailer truck down state about 200 miles and we brought almost ten tons of stock to Chicago market.

He had told me where we were going and I had to figure out the highways to take and also the mileage. He didn't do anything but drive and turn where I told him to. Was that fun! I sat with a map in my lap and told him to turn south or southeast or some other direction. We made seven stops and drove over 500 miles round trip. I'm figuring now what his oil cost and also the wear and tear on the truck—he calls it depreciation—so we'll know how much we made.

I even write out all the bills and send letters to the farmers about what their pigs and beef cattle brought at the stockyards. I only made three mistakes in 17 letters last time, my aunt said—all commas. She's been through high school and reads them over. I wish I could write school themes that way. The last one I had to write was on, "What a Daffodil Thinks of Spring," and I just couldn't get going.

I don't do very well in school in arithmetic either. Seems I just can't keep my mind on the problems. We had one the other day like this:

If a 57 foot telephone pole falls across the cement highway so that $17\frac{3}{6}$ feet extend from one side and $14\frac{9}{17}$ from the other, how wide is the highway?

That seemed to me like an awfully silly way to get the width of a highway. I didn't even try to answer it because it didn't say whether the pole had fallen straight across or not.

### NOT GETTING ANY YOUNGER

Even in shop I don't get very good marks. All of us kids made a broom holder and bookend this term and mine were sloppy. I just couldn't get interested. Mom doesn't use a broom any more with her new vacuum cleaner and all our books are in a bookcase with glass doors in the parlor. Anyway, I wanted to make an end gate for my uncle's trailer but the shop teacher said that meant using metal and wood both and I'd have to learn how to work with wood first. I didn't see why but I kept still and made a tie rack at school and the tail gate after school at my uncle's garage. He said I saved him $10.

Civics is hard for me, too. I've been staying after school trying to learn the "Articles of Confederation" for almost a week because the teacher said we couldn't be good citizens unless we did. I really tried, because I want to be a good citizen. I did hate to stay after school, though, because a bunch of us boys from the south end of town have been cleaning up the old lot across from Taylor's Machine Shop to make a playground out of it for the little kids from the Methodist Home. I made the jungle gym from old pipe and the guys made me Grand Mogul to keep the playground going. We raised enough money collecting scrap this month to build a wire fence clear around the lot.

Dad says I can quit school when I'm fifteen and I'm sort of anxious to because there a lot of things I want to learn how to do and as my uncle says, I'm not getting any younger.

---

**What Do You Think?**

1.  The article you just read was called "Poor Scholar's Soliloquy." How do you think a "good scholar" would respond to this article?

2.  Some people would say that the conditions described above

also exist in colleges and universities. What evidence can you cite that supports that view? That contradicts it?

3.    What does this reading tell you about the causes of alienation?

## 2. THE ROOTS OF OUR MALADY *

*In the next reading, the author takes a look at several sweeping changes that have occurred in western civilization over the past one hundred years. These changes, he believes, have played a major role in the alienation of many Americans. What evidence does he offer to support his position?*

One of the two central beliefs in the modern period since the Renaissance has been in the value of individual competition. The conviction was that the more a man worked to further his own economic self-interest and to become wealthy, the more he would contribute to the material progress of the community. This famous laissez-faire theory in economics worked well for several centuries. It *was* true through the early and growing stages of modern industrialism and capitalism that for you or me to strive to become rich by increasing our trade or building a bigger factory would eventually mean the production of more material goods for the community. The pursuit of competitive enterprise was a magnificent and courageous idea in its heyday. But in the nineteenth and twentieth centuries considerable changes occurred. In our present day of giant business and monopoly capitalism how many people can become successful *individual* competitors? There are very few groups left who, like doctors and psychotherapists and some farmers, still have the luxury of being their own economic bosses—and even they are subject to the rise and fall of prices and the fluctuating market like everyone else. The vast majority of workingmen and capitalists alike, professional people or businessmen, must fit into broad groups such as labor unions or big industries or university systems, or they would not survive economically at all. We have been taught to strive to get ahead of the next man, but actually today one's success depends much more on how well one learns to work with one's fellow workers. I have just read that even the individual crook cannot make out very well on his own these days: he has to join a racket!

\*    \*    \*    \*    \*

If you or I had a farm to carve out of the frontier forest two centuries ago, or possessed a little capital with which to start a new business

---

\* Reprinted from *Man's Search for Himself* by Rollo May, Ph.D. By permission of W. W. Norton & Company, Inc. Copyright 1953 by W. W. Norton & Company, Inc.

last century, the philosophy of "each man for himself" would have brought out the best in us and resulted in the best for the community. But how does such competitive individualism work in a day when even corporation wives are screened to fit the "pattern"?

The individual's striving for his own gain, in fine, without an equal emphasis on social welfare, no longer automatically brings good to the community. Furthermore, this type of individual competitiveness—in which for you to fail in a deal is as good as for me to succeed, since it pushes me ahead in the scramble up the ladder—raises many psychological problems. It makes every man the potential enemy of his neighbor, it generates much interpersonal hostility and resentment, and increases greatly our anxiety and isolation from each other. As this hostility has come closer to the surface in recent decades, we have tried to cover it up by various devices—by becoming "joiners" of all sorts of service organizations, from Rotary to Optimist Clubs in the 1920's and 30's, by being good fellows, well-liked by all, and so on. But the conflicts sooner or later burst forth into the open.

This is pictured beautifully and tragically in Willie Loman, the chief character in Arthur Miller's *Death of a Salesman*. Willie had been taught, and in turn taught his sons, that to get ahead of the next fellow and to get rich were the goals, and this required initiative. When the boys steal balls and lumber, Willie, though he pays lip-service to the idea that he should rebuke them, is pleased that they are "fearless characters" and remarks that the "coach will probably congratulate them on their initiative." His friend reminds him that the jails are full of "fearless characters," but Willie rejoins, "the stock exchange is, too."

Willie tries to cover up his competitiveness, like most men of two or three decades ago, by being "well-liked." When as an old man he is "cast into the ash can" by virtue of the changing policies of his company, Willie is caught in great bewilderment, and keeps repeating to himself, "But I was the best-liked." His confusion in this conflict of values—why does what he was taught not work?—mounts up until it culminates in his suicide. At the grave one son continues to insist, "He had a good dream, to come out number one." But the other son accurately sees the contradiction which such an upheaval of values leads to, "He never knew who he was." . . .

Some readers may be thinking that many of the above questions are stated wrongly—why does economic striving need to be *against* one's fellow men, and why reason *against* emotion? True, but the characteristic of a period of change like the present is precisely that everyone does ask the wrong questions. The old goals, criteria, principles are still there in our minds and "habits," but they do not fit, and hence most people are eternally frustrated by asking questions which never could lead to the right answer. Or they become lost in a potpourri [1] of contradictory answers—"reason" operates while one goes to class, "emotion" when one visits one's lover, "will power" when one studies for an exam, and religious duty at funerals and on Easter Sunday. This compartmentalization of values and goals leads very quickly to an undermining of the unity of the personality, and the person, in "pieces" within as well as without, does not know which way to go.

\*     \*     \*     \*     \*

The upshot is that the values and goals which provided a unifying center for previous centuries in the modern period no longer are cogent.[2] We have not yet found the new center which will enable us to choose our goals constructively, and thus to overcome the painful bewilderment and anxiety of not knowing which way to move.

### THE LOSS OF THE SENSE OF SELF

Another root of our malady is our loss of the sense of the worth and dignity of the human being. Nietzsche [3] predicted this when he pointed out that the individual was being swallowed up in the herd, and that we were living by a "slave-morality." Marx also predicted it when he proclaimed that modern man was being "de-humanized," and Kafka showed in his amazing stories how people literally can lose their identity as persons.

\*     \*     \*     \*     \*

Along with the loss of the sense of self has gone a loss of our language for communicating deeply personal meanings to each other. This is one important side of the loneliness now experienced by people in the Western world. Take the word "love" for example, a word which obviously should be most important in conveying personal feelings. When you use it, the person you are talking to may think you mean Hollywood love, or the sentimental emotion of the popular songs, "I love my baby, my baby loves me," or religious charity, or friendliness, or sexual impulse, or whatnot. The same is true about almost any other important word in the nontechnical area—"truth," "integrity," "courage," "spirit," "freedom," and even the word "self." Most people have private connotations for such words which may be quite different from their neighbor's meaning, and hence some people even try to avoid using such words.

We have an excellent vocabulary for technical subjects, as Erich Fromm has pointed out; almost every man can name the parts of an auto-

---

[1] a miscellaneous collection
[2] valid
[3] German philosopher (1844–1900)

mobile engine clearly and definitely. But when it comes to meaningful interpersonal relations, our language is lost: we stumble, and are practically as isolated as deaf and dumb people who can only communicate in sign language. . . .

This loss of the effectiveness of language, it may seem strange to point out, is a symptom of a disrupted historical period. . . . I believe it could be shown in researches—which obviously cannot be gone into here—that when a culture is in its historical phase of growing toward unity, its language reflects the unity and power; whereas when a culture is in the process of change, dispersal and disintegration, the language likewise loses its power.

---

**What Do You Think?**

1. Dr. May says that in a period of change—"like the present"— people tend to ask the "wrong questions." How would asking the wrong questions contribute to one's alienation? What might some "right questions" be?

2. He also says that "when a culture is in the process of change, dispersal and disintegration, the language . . . loses its power." Do you believe that our culture is in such a process? If not, what alternative explanation might you offer to replace that of the author?

## 3.   I AM WAITING *

*In the following poem, the poet is "waiting" for a large number of events to occur. In so doing, he is pointing to several aspects of modern life that he believes to be exerting alienating influences. As you read the poem, see if you can identify those alienating conditions.*

> I am waiting for my case to come up
> and I am waiting
> for a rebirth of wonder
> and I am waiting for someone
> to really discover America
> and wail
> and I am waiting
> for the discovery

---

* By Lawrence Ferlinghetti. "I Am Waiting" in *A Coney Island of the Mind.* Copyright © 1958 by Lawrence Ferlinghetti. Reprinted by permission of New Directions Publishing Corporation.

of a new symbolic western frontier
and I am waiting
for the American Eagle
to really spread its wings
and straighten up and fly right
and I am waiting
for the Age of Anxiety
to drop dead
and I am waiting
for the war to be fought
which will make the world safe
for anarchy
and I am waiting
for the final withering away
of all governments
and I am perpetually awaiting
a rebirth of wonder

I am waiting for the Second Coming
and I am waiting
for a religious revival
to sweep thru the state of Arizona
and I am waiting
for them to prove
that God is really American
and I am seriously waiting
for Billy Graham and Elvis Presley
to exchange roles seriously
and I am waiting
to see God on television
piped onto church altars
if only they can find
the right channel
to tune in on
and I am waiting
for the Last Supper to be served again
with a strange new appetizer
and I am perpetually awaiting
a rebirth of wonder

I am waiting for my number to be called
and I am waiting
for the living end
and I am waiting
for dad to come home

his pockets full
of irradiated silver dollars
and I am waiting
for the atomic tests to end
and I am waiting happily
for things to get much worse
before they improve
and I am waiting
for the Salvation Army to take over
and I am waiting
for the human crowd
to wander off a cliff somewhere
clutching its atomic umbrella
and I am waiting
for Ike to act
and I am waiting
for the meek to be blessed
and inherit the earth
without taxes
and I am waiting
for forests and animals
to reclaim the earth as theirs
and I am waiting
for a way to be devised
to destroy all nationalisms
without killing anybody
and I am waiting
for linnets and planets to fall like rain
and I am waiting for lovers and weepers
to lie down together again
in a new rebirth of wonder

I am waiting for the Great Divide to be crossed
and I am anxiously waiting
for the secret of eternal life to be discovered
by an obscure general practitioner
and save me forever from certain death
and I am waiting
for life to begin
and I am waiting
for the storms of life
to be over
and I am waiting
to set sail for happiness

and I am waiting
for a reconstructed Mayflower
to reach America
with its picture story and tv rights
sold in advance to the natives
and I am waiting
for the lost music to sound again
in the Lost Continent
in a new rebirth of wonder

I am waiting for the day
that maketh all things clear
and I am waiting
for Ole Man River
to just stop rolling along
past the country club
and I am waiting
for the deepest South
to just stop Reconstructing itself
in its own image
and I am waiting
for a sweet desegrated chariot
to swing low
and carry me back to Ole Virginie
and I am waiting
for Ole Virginie to discover
just why Darkies are born . . .

---

**What Do You Think?**

1. In what ways is Ferlinghetti's position similar to that expressed by Rollo May in "The Roots of Our Malady"? In what ways do the two men differ? Cite evidence to support your view.

2. The poem was written during the Eisenhower Administration ("waiting for Ike to act"). Have any of the events for which the poet is waiting taken place? Have any conditions changed? Explain.

## 4. BUREAUCRACY: THE IMPERSONAL GIANT *

*It has been said that for many Americans, bigness is the equivalent of greatness. The next selection provides a brief glimpse of the "other side of the coin."*

The manager, like the worker, like everybody, deals with impersonal giants: with the giant competitive enterprise; with the giant national and world market; with the giant consumer, who has to be coaxed and manipulated; with the giant unions, and the giant government. All these giants have their own lives, as it were. They determine the activity of the manager and they direct the activity of the worker and clerk.

The problem of the manager opens up one of the most significant phenomena in an alienated culture, that of *bureaucratization*. Both big business and government administrations are conducted by a bureaucracy. Bureaucrats are specialists in the administration of things *and of men*. Due to the bigness of the apparatus to be administered, and the resulting abstractification, the bureaucrats' relationship to the people is one of complete alienation. They, the people to be administered, are objects whom the bureaucrats consider neither with love nor with hate, but completely impersonally; the manager-bureaucrat must not feel, as far as his professional activity is concerned; he must manipulate people as though they were figures, or things. Since the vastness of the organization and the extreme division of labor prevents any single individual from seeing the whole, since there is no organic, spontaneous co-operation between the various individuals or groups within the industry, the managing bureaucrats are necessary; without them the enterprise would collapse in a short time, since nobody would know the secret which makes it function. Bureaucrats are as indispensable as the tons of paper consumed under their leadership. Just because everybody senses, with a feeling of powerlessness, the vital role of the bureaucrats, they are given an almost godlike respect. If it were not for the bureaucrats, people feel, everything would go to pieces, and we would starve. Whereas, in the medieval world, the leaders were considered representatives of a god-intended order, in modern Capitalism the role of the bureaucrat is hardly less sacred—since he is necessary for the survival of the whole.

Marx gave a profound definition of the bureaucrat saying: "The bureaucrat relates himself to the world as a *mere object* of his activity."

---

* Excerpted from Erich Fromm, *The Sane Society,* New York, N. Y.: Holt, Rinehart and Winston, 1955. Copyright © 1955 by Erich Fromm. Reprinted by permission of Holt, Rinehart and Winston, Inc.

It is interesting to note that the spirit of bureaucracy has entered not only business and government administration, but also trade unions and the great democratic socialist parties in England, Germany and France. In Russia, too, the bureaucratic managers and their alienated spirit have conquered the country. Russia could perhaps exist without terror—if certain conditions were given—but it could not exist without the system. of total bureaucratization—that is alienation.

---

**What Do You Think?**

1. Nearly everyone comes into contact with a number of large organizations as he goes about the business of living in America today. From your own experience, cite some examples of impersonal treatment by "bureaucrats." Cite some examples of "personal" treatment by members of a bureaucracy. How might such "impersonal" treatment be turned into "personal" treatment?

2. Does the evidence of your own experience support or contradict Fromm's position?

## 5. THE GREAT EMPTINESS *

*The creation of large organizations, however, has played a major role in the reduction of the length of the working day for many Americans. The next article deals with the paradox that the freeing of people's time for leisure itself exerts an alienating influence on many of those people.*

"In the sweat of thy face shalt thou eat bread." From this primal decree millions of human beings are now liberated. More and more men have more and more leisure. The working day grows shorter, the week end longer. More and more women are released at an earlier age from the heavier tasks of the rearing of children, in the small family of today, when kindergarten and school and clinic and restaurant come to their aid. More and more people are freed for other things, released from the exhaustion of their energies in the mere satisfaction of elementary wants.
. . .

Released for what? When necessity no longer drives, when people own long hours in which to do what they want, what do they want to

---

* Excerpted from R. M. MacIver, *The Pursuit of Happiness,* New York, N. Y.: Simon and Schuster, 1955. Copyright © 1955 by R. M. MacIver. Reprinted by permission of Simon and Schuster.

do? Where necessity is heavy upon men, they yearn for the joys of leisure. Now many have enough leisure. What are the joys they find? . . .

It is a marvelous liberation for those who learn to use it; and there are many ways. It is the great emptiness for those who don't.

People of a placid disposition do not know the great emptiness. When the day's work is done, they betake themselves to their quiet interests, their hobbies, their garden or their amateur workbenches or their stamp collecting or their games or their social affairs or their church activities or whatever it be. When they need more sting in life, they have a mild "fling," taking a little "moral holiday." Some find indulgence enough in the vicarious pleasure of snidely malicious gossip. Their habits are early formed and they keep a modicum of contentment.

But the number of the placid is growing less. The conditions of our civilization do not encourage that mood. For one thing, the oldtime acceptance of authority, as God-given or nature-based, is much less common. Religion is for very many an ancient tale, "a tale of little meaning, though the words are strong," reduced to ritual or the moral precepts of the Sunday pulpit. There is little allegiance to the doctrine that every man has his allotted place. How could there be when competition has become a law of life? There is incessant movement and disturbance and upheaval. And with the new leisure there come new excitations, new stimuli to unrest.

So the new leisure has brought its seeming opposite, restlessness. And because these cannot be reconciled the great emptiness comes.

Faced with the great emptiness, unprepared to meet it, most people resort to one or another way of escape, according to their kind. Those who are less conscious of their need succeed in concealing it from themselves. They find their satisfaction in the great new world of means without ends. Those who are more conscious of it cannot conceal it; they only distract themselves from the thought of it. Their common recourse is excitation, and they seek it in diverse ways.

The first kind are go-getters. When they are efficient or unscrupulous or both, they rise in the world. They amass things. They make some money. They win some place and power. Not *for* anything, not to do anything with it. Their values are relative, which means they are no values at all. They make money to make more money. They win some power that enables them to seek more power. They are practical men. They keep right on being practical, until their unlived lives are at an end. If they stopped being practical, the great emptiness would engulf them. They are like planes that must keep on flying because they have no landing gear. The engines go fast and faster, but they are going nowhere. They make good progress to nothingness.

They take pride in their progress. They are outdistancing other men. They are always calculating the distance they have gained. It shows what can be done when you have the know-how. They feel superior and that sustains them. They stay assured in the world of means. What matters is the winning.

> "But what good came of it at last?"
> Quoth little Peterkin.
> "Why that I cannot tell," said he,
> "But 'twas a famous victory."

Victory for the sake of the winning, means for the sake of the acquiring, that is success. So the circle spins forever, means without end, world without end. Amen.

The second kind have it worse. They are the more sensitive kind, often the more gifted. They want their lives to have some meaning, some fulfillment. They want the feel of living for some worthwhile end. But often there is something wrong with the seeking. They too suffer from the intrusive ego. Their seeking lacks adequate sincerity. The need of success is greater for them than the need of the thing that is sought. If, for example, they pursue some art, the art itself counts less than the renown of the artist. They would be great artists, great writers, opera singers, pathfinders. They aim high, but the mark is higher than their reach. When they miss it they grow disillusioned. They are thrust back on their unsatisfied egos, and the great emptiness lies before them.

\*　　\*　　\*　　\*　　\*

But it is not only the more cultivated, the more sophisticated, and the well-to-do with their more ample opportunities, who feel the great emptiness. In other ways it besets large numbers who, finding little satisfaction in their daily work, seek compensation in the leisure they now possess. There are many besides, people who win early pensions or otherwise can get along without toil through legacies or rents or other sources of unearned income, women who have no family cares—the new, unopulent leisure class.

They have no training for leisure. They have, most of them, no strong interests or devotions. The habits of their work time convey no meaning to the time of liberation. Most of them live in cities, in drab and narrow confines within which they revolve in casual little circles. They see nothing ahead but the coming of old age. They want to regain the feel of life. Time is theirs, but they cannot redeem it.

So they betake themselves, in their various ways, to some form of excitation. Having no recourse in themselves, they must get out of themselves. They take the easy ways out because they see no alternative. They have never learned to climb the paths leading to the pleasures that wait in the realm of ideas, in the growing revelation of the nature of things, in the treasuries of the arts, and in the rich lore of the libraries. They must seek instead the quick transport, the dreams, the adventure, in the tavern or where the gamblers meet.

They would cover the emptiness they cannot fill. They make a goal of what is a diversion. The healthy being craves an occasional wildness, a jolt from normality, a sharpening of the edge of appetite, . . . a brief excursion from his way of life. But for these others the diversion becomes the way of life and diverts no more. For them the filled glass is not the cheerful accompaniment of pleasant reunions but a deceitful medicine for the ennui of living. For them the gambling venture is no mere holiday flutter but a never-satisfied urge that forever defeats itself.

In 1946, in straitened England, the then equivalent of half a billion dollars was placed in bets on the horses and the dogs. Besides which, vast sums changed hands on the results of football games. For hundreds of thousands of people the major news in the daily papers, day after day and month after month, was the lists of the winners and the betting odds. England was not, is not, alone in this respect. It is only that the figures happen to be more accessible.

A former addict explained in the London *Spectator* why men do it. The gambler, he said, "gambles because it provides an emotional tension which his mind demands. He is suffering from a deficiency disease, and the only antidote he knows is gambling." He is trying to escape the great emptiness. An English worker of the semi-skilled category once said to me: "A fellow had to do something, and what is there? Maybe I have a shilling or two in my pocket. Maybe I could buy an extra shirt. It's no go. So I put them on the dogs."

By these resorts people do not escape the great emptiness. What they get is a sequence of brief delusions of escape. In time the only thing they can escape to is what they themselves know for a delusion. The resort is only a drug to make them forget the disease. As with all such drugs, the dose must be continually renewed, and it becomes harder and harder to return to the pre-addict stage. They come to look on the great emptiness as something inherent in the very nature of things. That is all life is. Now they know the drug is a delusion, but they do not know that it has bred a deeper delusion.

\*     \*     \*     \*     \*

Back in the days when unremitting toil was the lot of all but the very few and leisure still a hopeless yearning, hard and painful as life was, it still felt real. People were in *rapport* with the small bit of reality allotted to them, the sense of the earth, the tang of the changing seasons, the consciousness of the eternal on-going of birth and death. Now, when so many have leisure, they become detached from themselves, not merely from the earth. . . . The leisure is ours but not the skill to use it. So leisure becomes a void, and from the ensuing restlessness men take refuge in delusive excitations or fictitious visions returning to their own earth no more.

---

1.  MacIver seems to be saying that some uses of leisure time are "better" than others. Do you agree or disagree?
2.  What criteria do you think MacIver might use to evaluate uses of leisure time? Find statements in the article to support your answer.
3.  What criteria would you suggest be used to evaluate the use of leisure?

### 6. 🕇 THE SOCIAL ASPECT OF WORK *

*Many people believe that the monotony of work on the modern assembly line is a prime contributor to the alienation of the workers on the line. The following report of a study conducted with assembly line workers suggests that the answer is not quite that simple.*

. . . [A] by now classic experiment [was] carried out by Elton Mayo at the Chicago Hawthorne Works of the Western Electric Company. The operation selected was that of assembling telephone coils, work which ranks as a repetitive performance, and is usually performed by women. A standard assembly bench with the appropriate equipment, and with places for five women workers, was put into a room, which was separated by a partition from the main assembly room; altogether six operatives worked in this room, five working at the bench, and one distributing parts to those engaged in the assembly. All of the women were experienced workers. Two of them dropped out within the first year, and their places were taken by two other workers of equal skill. Altogether, the experiment lasted for five years, and was divided into various experimental periods, in which certain changes were made in the conditions of work. Without going into the details of these changes, it suffices to state that rest pauses were adopted in the morning and afternoon, refreshments offered during these rest pauses, and the hours of work cut by half an hour. Throughout these changes, the output of each worker rose considerably. So far, so good; nothing was more plausible than the assumption that increased rest periods and some attempt to make the worker

---

* Excerpted from Erich Fromm, *The Sane Society,* New York, N. Y.: Holt, Rinehart, and Winston, 1955. Copyright © 1955 by Erich Fromm. Reprinted by permission of Holt, Rinehart and Winston, Inc.

"feel better" were the cause for an increased efficiency. But a new arrangement in the twelfth experimental period disappointed this expectation and showed rather dramatic results: by arrangement with the workers, the group returned to the conditions of work as they had existed in the beginning of the experiment. Rest periods, special refreshments, and other improvements were all abolished for approximately three months. To everybody's amazement this did not result in a *decrease* of output but, on the contrary, the daily and weekly output rose to a higher point than at any time before. In the next period, the old concessions were introduced again, with the only exception that the girls provided their own food, while the company continued to supply coffee for the mid-morning lunch. The output still continued to rise. And not only the output. What is equally important is the fact that the rate of sickness among the workers in this experiment fell by about 80 per cent in comparison with the general rate, and that a new social friendly intercourse developed among the working women participating in the experiment.

How can we explain the surprising result that "the steady increase seemed to ignore the experimental changes in its upward development"? If it was not the rest pauses, the tea, the shortened working time, what was it that made the workers produce more, be more healthy and more friendly among themselves? The answer is obvious: while the *technical* aspect of monotonous, uninteresting work remained the same, and while even certain improvements like rest pauses were not decisive, the *social* aspect of the total work situation had changed, and caused a change in the attitude of the workers. They were informed of the experiment, and of the several steps in it; their suggestions were listened to and often followed, and what is perhaps the most important point, they were aware of participating in a meaningful and interesting experiment, which was important not only to themselves, but to the workers of the whole factory. While they were at first "shy and uneasy, silent and perhaps somewhat suspicious of the company's intentions," later their attitude was marked "by confidence and candor." The group developed a sense of participation in the work, because they knew what they were doing, they had an aim and purpose, and they could influence the whole procedure by their suggestions.

The startling results of Mayo's experiment show that sickness, fatigue and a resulting low output are not caused primarily by the monotonous *technical* aspect of the work, but by the alienation of the worker from the total work situation in its social aspects.

---

**What Do You Think?**

Compare Fromm's emphasis on the alienating influences of the social aspects of work with the comments made by workers and reported in the selection on "The Man on the Assembly Line" in Chapter 3. Which of those statements support Fromm's position? Which do not? Explain.

## 7. GROWING UP BLACK *

*The final two selections in this chapter explore, from different perspectives, conditions that contribute to the alienation of black Americans from American society. In the first of these selections, Malcolm X recounts one of his experiences as he grew up in a small town in Michigan.*

That summer of 1940, in Lansing, I caught the Greyhound bus for Boston with my cardboard suitcase, and wearing my green suit. If someone had hung a sign, "HICK," around my neck, I couldn't have looked much more obvious. They didn't have the turnpikes then; the bus stopped at what seemed every corner and cowpatch. From my seat in—you guessed it—the back of the bus, I gawked out of the window at white man's America rolling past for what seemed a month, but must have been only a day and a half.

When we finally arrived, Ella met me at the terminal and took me home. The house was on Waumbeck Street in the Sugar Hill section of Roxbury, the Harlem of Boston. I met Ella's second husband, Frank, who was now a soldier; and her brother Earl, the singer who called himself Jimmy Carleton; and Mary, who was very different from her older sister. It's funny how I seemed to think of Mary as Ella's sister, instead of her being, just as Ella is, my own half-sister. It's probably because Ella and I always were much closer as basic types; we're dominant people, and Mary has always been mild and quiet, almost shy.

Ella was busily involved in dozens of things. She belonged to I don't know how many different clubs; she was a leading light of local so-called "black society." I saw and met a hundred black people there whose big-city talk and ways left my mouth hanging open.

I couldn't have feigned indifference if I had tried to. People talked casually about Chicago, Detroit, New York. I didn't know the world contained as many Negroes as I saw thronging downtown Roxbury at night, especially on Saturdays. Neon lights, nightclubs, poolhalls, bars, the cars they drove! Restaurants made the streets smell—rich, greasy, down-home black cooking! Jukeboxes blared Erskine Hawkins, Duke Ellington, Cootie Williams, dozens of others. If somebody had told me

* Excerpted from Alex Haley and Malcolm X, *The Autobiography of Malcolm X,* New York, N. Y.: Grove Press, 1964. Reprinted by permission of Grove Press, Inc. Copyright © 1964 by Alex Haley and Malcolm X. Copyright 1965 by Alex Haley and Betty Shabazz.

then that some day I'd know them all personally, I'd have found it hard to believe. The biggest bands, like these, played at the Roseland State Ballroom, on Boston's Massachusetts Avenue—one night for Negroes, the next night for whites.

I saw for the first time occasional black-white couples strolling around arm in arm. And on Sundays, when Ella, Mary, or somebody took me to church, I saw churches for black people such as I had never seen. They were many times finer than the white church I had attended back in Mason, Michigan. There, the white people just sat and worshiped with words; but the Boston Negroes, like all other Negroes I had ever seen at church, threw their souls and bodies wholly into worship.

Two or three times, I wrote letters to Wilfred intended for everybody back in Lansing. I said I'd try to describe it when I got back.

But I found I couldn't.

My restlessness with Mason—and for the first time in my life a restlessness with being around white people—began as soon as I got back home and entered eighth grade.

I continued to think constantly about all that I had seen in Boston, and about the way I had felt there. I know now that it was the sense of being a real part of a mass of my own kind, for the first time.

The white people—classmates, the Swerlins, the people at the restaurant where I worked—noticed the change. They said, "You're acting so strange. You don't seem like yourself, Malcolm. What's the matter?"

I kept close to the top of the class, though. The top-most scholastic standing, I remember, kept shifting between me, a girl named Audrey Slaugh, and a boy named Jimmy Cotton.

It went on that way, as I became increasingly restless and disturbed through the first semester. And then one day, just about when those of us who had passed were about to move up to 8-A, from which we would enter high school the next year, something happened which was to become the first major turning point of my life.

Somehow, I happened to be alone in the classroom with Mr. Ostrowski, my English teacher. He was a tall, rather reddish white man and he had a thick mustache. I had gotten some of my best marks under him, and he had always made me feel that he liked me. He was, as I have mentioned, a natural-born "advisor," about what you ought to read, to do, or think—about any and everything. We used to make unkind jokes about him: why was he teaching in Mason instead of somewhere else, getting for himself some of the "success in life" that he kept telling us how to get?

I know that he probably meant well in what he happened to advise me that day. I doubt that he meant any harm. It was just in his nature as an American white man. I was one of his top students, one of the school's top students—but all he could see for me was the kind of future "in your place" that almost all white people see for black people.

He told me, "Malcolm, you ought to be thinking about a career. Have you been giving it thought?"

The truth is, I hadn't. I never have figured out why I told him, "Well, yes, sir, I've been thinking I'd like to be a lawyer." Lansing certainly had no Negro lawyers—or doctors either—in those days, to hold up an image I might have aspired to. All I really knew for certain was that a lawyer didn't wash dishes, as I was doing.

Mr. Ostrowski looked surprised, I remember, and leaned back in his chair and clasped his hands behind his head. He kind of half-smiled and said, "Malcolm, one of life's first needs is for us to be realistic. Don't misunderstand me, now. We all here like you, you know that. But you've got to be realistic about being a nigger. A lawyer—that's no realistic goal for a nigger. You need to thing about something you *can* be. You're good with your hands—making things. Everybody admires your carpentry shop work. Why don't you plan on carpentry? People like you as a person—you'd get all kinds of work."

The more I thought afterwards about what he said, the more uneasy it made me. It just kept treading around in my mind.

What made it really begin to disturb me was Mr. Ostrowski's advice to others in my class—all of them white. Most of them had told him they were planning to become farmers. But those who wanted to strike out on their own, to try something new, he had encouraged. Some, mostly girls, wanted to be teachers. A few wanted other professions, such as one boy who wanted to become a county agent; another, a veterinarian; and one girl wanted to be a nurse. They all reported that Mr. Ostrowski had encouraged what they had wanted. Yet nearly none of them had earned marks equal to mine.

It was a surprising thing that I had never thought of it that way before, but I realized that whatever I wasn't, I *was* smarter than nearly all of those white kids. But apparently I was still not intelligent enough, in their eyes, to become whatever *I* wanted to be.

It was then that I began to change—inside.

I drew away from white people. I came to class, and I answered when called upon. It became a physical strain simply to sit in Mr. Ostrowski's class.

Where "nigger" had slipped off my back before, wherever I heard it now, I stopped and looked at whoever said it. And they looked surprised that I did.

---

### What Do You Think?

Malcolm's encounter with his English teacher was a rather open and direct one. Can you think of any more subtle or covert situations that might have a similar impact? If you are black, perhaps you can point to such experiences in your own life.

## 8. RACIAL DISORDER: WHY DID IT HAPPEN? *

*Following the summer of 1967, in which there were numerous up-risings and disorders in the ghetto areas of our larger cities, President Lyndon Johnson appointed a National Commission on Civil Disorders. The task of that Commission was to explore carefully those disorders and the reasons for their occurrence. The following section is taken from the Report of that Commission.*

The record before this Commission reveals that the causes of recent racial disorders are imbedded in a massive tangle of issues and circumstances—social, economic, political, and psychological—which arise out of the historical pattern of Negro-white relations in America.

These factors are both complex and interacting; they vary significantly in their effect from city to city and from year to year; and the consequences of one disorder, generating new grievances and new demands, become the causes of the next. It is this which creates the "thicket of tension, conflicting evidence and extreme opinions" cited by the President.

Despite these complexities, certain fundamental matters are clear. Of these, the most fundamental is the racial attitude and behavior of white Americans toward black Americans. Race prejudice has shaped our history decisively in the past; it now threatens to do so again. White racism is essentially responsible for the explosive mixture which has been accumulating in our cities since the end of World War II. At the base of this mixture are three of the most bitter fruits of white racial attitudes:

*Pervasive discrimination and segregation.* The first is surely the continuing exclusion of great numbers of Negroes from the benefits of economic progress through discrimination in employment and education, and their enforced confinement in segregated housing and schools. The corrosive and degrading effects of this condition and the attitudes that underlie it are the source of the deepest bitterness and at the center of the problem of racial disorder.

*Black migration and white exodus.* The second is the massive and growing concentration of impoverished Negroes in our major cities resulting from Negro migration from the rural South, rapid population growth and the continuing movement of the white middle-class to the

---

* Excerpted from the *Report of the National Advisory Commission on Civil Disorders,* U. S. Government Printing Office, Washington, D. C., 1968.

suburbs. The consequence is a greatly increased burden on the already depleted resources of cities, creating a growing crisis of deteriorating facilities and services and unmet human needs.

*Black ghettos.* Third, in the teeming racial ghettos, segregation and poverty have intersected to destroy opportunity and hope and to enforce failure. The ghettos too often mean men and women without jobs, families without men, and schools where children are processed instead of educated, until they return to the street—to crime, to narcotics, to dependency on welfare, and to bitterness and resentment against society in general and white society in particular.

These three forces have converged on the inner city in recent years and on the people who inhabit it. At the same time, most whites and many Negroes outside the ghetto have prospered to a degree unparalleled in the history of civilization. Through television—the universal appliance in the ghetto—and the other media of mass communications, this affluence has been endlessly flaunted before the eyes of the Negro poor and the jobless ghetto youth.

As Americans, most Negro citizens carry within themselves two basic aspirations of our society. They seek to share in both the material resources of our system and its intangible benefits—dignity, respect and acceptance. Outside the ghetto many have succeeded in achieving a decent standard of life, and in developing the inner resources which give life meaning and direction. Within the ghetto, however, it is rare that either aspiration is achieved.

Yet these facts alone—fundamental as they are—cannot be said to have caused the disorders. Other and more immediate factors help explain why these events happened now.

Recently, three powerful ingredients have begun to catalyze the mixture.

*Frustrated hopes.* The expectations aroused by the great judicial and legislative victories of the civil rights movement have led to frustration, hostility and cynicism in the face of the persistent gap between promise and fulfillment. The dramatic struggle for equal rights in the South has sensitized Northern Negroes to the economic inequalities reflected in the deprivations of ghetto life.

*Legitimation of violence.* A climate that tends toward the approval and encouragement of violence as a form of protest has been created by white terrorism directed against nonviolent protest, including instances of abuse and even murder of some civil rights workers in the South; by the open defiance of law and federal authority by state and local officials resisting desegregation; and by some protest groups engaging in civil disobedience who turn their backs on nonviolence, go beyond the Constitutionally protected rights of petition and free assembly, and resort to violence to attempt to compel alteration of laws and policies with which they disagree. This condition has been reinforced by a general erosion of respect for authority in American society and reduced effectiveness of social standards and community restraints on violence and crime. This in turn has largely resulted from rapid urbanization and the dramatic reduction in the average age of the total population.

*Powerlessness.* Finally, many Negroes have come to believe that they are being exploited politically and economically by the white "power structure." Negroes, like people in poverty everywhere, in fact lack the channels of communication, influence and appeal that traditionally have been available to ethnic minorities within the city and which enabled them—unburdened by color—to scale the walls of the white ghettos in an earlier era. The frustrations of powerlessness have led some to the conviction that there is no effective alternative to violence as a means of expression and redress, as a way of "moving the system." More generally, the result is alienation and hostility toward the institutions of law and government and the white society which controls them. This is reflected in the reach toward racial consciousness and solidarity reflected in the slogan "Black Power."

These facts have combined to inspire a new mood among Negroes, particularly among the young. Self-esteem and enhanced racial pride are replacing apathy and submission to "the system." Moreover, Negro youth, who make up over half of the ghetto population, share the growing sense of alienation felt by many white youth in our country. Thus, their role in recent civil disorders reflects not only a shared sense of deprivation and victimization by white society but also the rising incidence of disruptive conduct by a segment of American youth throughout the society.

*Incitement and encouragement of violence.* These conditions have created a volatile mixture of attitudes and beliefs which needs only a spark to ignite mass violence. Strident appeals to violence, first heard from white racists, were echoed and reinforced last summer in the inflammatory rhetoric of black racists and militants. Throughout the year, extremists crisscrossed the country preaching a doctrine of black power and violence. Their rhetoric was widely reported in the mass media; it was echoed by local "militants" and organizations; it became the ugly background noise of the violent summer. . . .

*The police.* It is the convergence of all these factors that makes the role of the police so difficult and so significant. Almost invariably the incident that ignites disorder arises from police action. Harlem, Watts, Newark and Detroit—all the major outbursts of recent years—were precipitated by routine arrests of Negroes for minor offenses by white police.

But the police are not merely the spark. In discharge of their obligation to maintain order and insure public safety in the disruptive conditions of ghetto life, they are inevitably involved in sharper and more frequent conflicts with ghetto residents than with the residents of other areas. Thus, to many Negroes police have come to symbolize white power, white racism and white repression. And the fact is that many police do reflect and express these white attitudes. The atmosphere of hostility and cynicism is reinforced by a widespread perception among Negroes of the existence of police brutality and corruption, and of a "double standard" of justice and protection—one for Negroes and one for whites.

---

**What Do You Think?**

Review the sections of Chapter 3 that were written by black Americans. Which of those accounts support the conclusions of the Commission? Which do not?

## 9. THE PERMISSIVE SOCIETY *

*The explanations of the causes of alienation that you have read so far focus rather sharply on some of the basic institutions and structures of modern society. In contrast, the following selection finds the causes of the alienation of many young people in certain child-rearing ideas and practices of their elders. Do you agree with this writer's theories?*

Traditionally, one's parents function as the carriers of the positive values of a culture. The child absorbs those values through emulation. But he also defines himself, finds his identity and strengthens his ego, through his daily experience of parental authority: the authority and the will are there, and they must be reacted to, perhaps even reacted against. This process is a moral and psychological teething.

Our contemporary, middle-class, affluent college students have very largely been denied this experience. Growing up, they have inhabited a vast moral and psychological vacuum; in a sense, they have scarcely had any parents at all. Their comfortable, permissive affluent parents provided no authority, no defining resistance at all. They were "enlightened." They were "tolerant." They knew their Spock, their popular psychology . . . The thing they feared most was the child's disapproval, rather than the other way around. The last thing they wanted was to be "repressive." The result was that they transmitted very little positive culture at all. Neither through emulation nor collision could the child define himself.

---

* Excerpted from an editorial in the *National Review,* February 25, 1969. Reprinted from National Review, Inc., 150 East 35th Street, New York, New York 10016.

Father, at best, was a sort of friendly older child, and at worst a benign stooge. Mother was in the League of Women Voters.

The child was, of course, "loved." He was also . . . denied the necessary conditions of growth, of ego-development, of self-definition. A number of observers, in fact, have noticed the striking similarity between "protest" behavior and the manners of infantile rebellion: lying down, going limp, physical dirtiness, spitting.

School and college served these youths no better, providing merely an extension of the parents' enlightened and tolerant vapidity. Once again no positive culture is transmitted: merely techniques, skills, methods, "courses." Nowhere does authority—historical, religious, even the authority of individual experience—assert any claims. In the past, education had as its goal the creation of some desirable mode of being: it transmitted an image of the self. Today, no image of the desirable is proposed, either to accept or reject. In the liberal arts and in the social sciences— and most campus disruption emanates from students and faculty in these areas—there are no agreed-upon goals. A course is offered merely because it occurs to someone to offer it. This pervasive incoherence is the inner meaning of the currently fashionable practice of seating students on college policy-making committees, of giving them a say in the curriculum, and so forth. The academy is in the process of disavowing even its claim to professional authority. The college once stood "in the place of the parents," *in loco parentis,* transmitting a positive culture; ironically enough, it stands today *in loco parentis* still, the perfect reflection of the modern liberal parents' moral emptiness.

The faculty, which ought to be the ultimate source of power and authority in a college is of course thoroughly liberalized and so defines itself through its negations. It is against "nationalism," it is against "militarism," it is against "repressive" forms of morality. It says no to ROTC, no to Vietnam, it passes rancorous resolutions. It is highly "moral"—but in a negative way, for its sense of its moral standing flows almost entirely from its critical stance toward the "dominant" society. The liberal faculty, the liberal teachers in secondary school, the liberal parents—the modern student grows up in the midst of a vast vacuity.

It is only when one sees how pervasive these negations are in enlightened, middle-class American culture that one perceives the true meaning of "trust no one over thirty." Finding no authority in his elders, the student seeks authority among his peers. He will do what they do, toe the line of fashions which dictate his dress, his manners, his attitudes. Some seek solace in a world made up of purely personal relations—prematurely domestic, shacking up though unmarried, taking drugs, seeking in the current phrase "meaningful" relationships (which turn out, relentlessly, to be meaningless). Others lash out at the negations, meeting moral cowardice with a desperate insolence: I act, therefore I am. They lock up the liberal dean, who has just abolished parietals and kicked ROTC off campus; they run up the red flag on the math building. Perhaps—the pathetic hope is implicit—the dean will provide some definition, some resistance. Alas, there is only emptiness: the permissive smile. Amnesty. Concessions. The rebellious student is consumed with rage. How is it possible not to hate such utter emptiness? The tolerant liberal culture defines itself as "open"—that is, value-less. The student understands the pun: the liberal culture is worthless.

---

### What Do You Think?

1. Restate the writer's position in your own words. What evidence can you think of that supports this position? That casts doubt on it?

2. How would Art Johnston and John Sinclair (see Chapter 3) respond to the writer? Give reasons to support your answer.

3. What kind of remedies would the writer of this selection be likely to suggest for the conditions he describes? Would you agree with these remedies?

### ACTIVITIES FOR INVOLVEMENT

1. Make a list of the alienating influences discussed in this chapter. Then review each of the readings in Chapter 3 and determine whether any of these influences seem to be operating in each case. For those cases of alienation that seem to be unaccounted for, offer your own explanation or interpretation. Be sure to supply the reasoning behind your analysis. Select a panel of students to report their findings to the class and compare your conclusions with theirs. How would you explain any differences?

2. Expose yourself and your classmates to some subtle discrimination. Single out a group of students (for example, all blonds or all students with blue eyes) and subject them to a brief period of systematic but special treatment. For example, you might seat them all at the back of the room, require them to use only certain building entrances, water fountains, etc., and speak disparagingly of the characteristics upon which the discrimination is based. Have those students report to the class on their reactions to this treatment—in particular, how they *felt*. Then hold a class discussion on why people feel the way they do when they receive certain kinds of treatment at the hands of others.

3. Using Readings 4, 5, and 6 as the basis, prepare a questionnaire and interview a random sample of several workers and managers in a local factory, business, or government agency regarding their relationships with their colleagues and with the organization in which they work.

4. Write an essay or a poem, or prepare a collage on the topic, "Alienating Influences in America Today."

5.    Based on your study of the readings in this chapter, write an essay on the following question: "Is Alienation Inevitable in Modern America?" Be sure that you explain your reasoning, no matter what your position on the question.

6.    Several of the readings in this chapter (as well as earlier ones) are excerpts from full-length books. From these sources select one book. After reading that book, write a review of it from the standpoint of your study of alienation so far. Share your views with your classmates by giving an oral presentation on your reactions to the book. Does the author suggest in any way how such alienation might be prevented? If so, how? If not, what suggestions can you offer?

7.    Listed below are a number of reasons that have been offered for alienation in today's world. Rank these in order, from most contributory (1) to least (12).
- The "bigness" of everything.
- Rootlessness of many people.
- Disruption of family life.
- Wine, women, and song.
- Impersonal nature of modern life.
- Greed.
- Envy.
- Fear.
- Irrevelance of much that is taught to us during our early years in school.
- Decline of the dignity of work.
- Loss of a sense of personal worth.
- Apathy and indifference on the part of many people.
- Permissive child-rearing practices.

What reasons would you add? Delete? Explain. Is there any combination of reasons that you think particularly explanatory? Why?

# 5

# How Can We Cope With Alienation?

Can alienation be eliminated from modern life? If not, can its impact be minimized? What steps might we, as individuals and as members of groups, take to begin dealing with our feelings of alienation and with the conditions out of which these feelings arise? The readings in this final chapter provide a variety of responses to the problems of alienation and alienating influences with which we are confronted. As you read each selection, consider whether or not the suggestions made would be likely to contribute to the amelioration of alienation in modern America.

## 1. WHEN SILENCE IS A CRIME *

*In the following article, a noted attorney makes a strong plea for new "Good Samaritan" laws as an antidote to citizen apathy and indifference as witnesses to criminal activity.*

Minding your own business is a virtue, but not when you are on the scene while another human being is criminally attacked. It is incredible that honorable people should turn their backs on fellow citizens who are fighting for their lives. Yet this is what happened during a series of particularly shocking recent crimes. These incidents caused a wave of criticism against "apathy," but we cannot let it go at that. Witnesses who are in a position to help stop crimes ought to be held legally accountable if they refuse to bestir themselves. This will require new laws; I

---

* Excerpted from Louis Nizer, "When Silence Is a Crime," *McCall's Magazine,* October 1964. Reprinted by permission of Brandt and Brandt.

believe they should be enacted. If we cannot be depended upon to be
Good Samaritans when there is a cry for aid, then we need laws to re-
mind us of our obligation to humanity.

Such a law might have saved a life on March 13, when Miss Catherine Genovese, 28 years old, was knifed to death on suburban Long Island,
New York, while 38 persons heard her screams but ignored them. . . .

All too frequently, such incidents involve defenseless women; but
even sturdy men are not immune. It was never reported in the press; but
Van Heflin, the distinguished actor told me that on a bright Sunday at
3:30 in the afternoon, he was walking in Central Park, in New York,
near Seventy-Second Street, when a group of hoodlums blocked his path,
rear and front. When he tried to get through, one of them pulled a switch
blade. Having once served in the Navy, Van Heflin knew some tricks of
defense. He kicked the assailant in a vulnerable spot and got away.
Dozens of people witnessed the incident. Not one moved to aid him or
even cried out for help.

Fortunately, the legal remedy against those who fail to aid a citizen
in distress is not at all complicated. The trouble is only that we have
not yet cared deeply enough to adopt it.

The doctrine of the Good Samaritan is not supported by law except
in North Carolina. Everywhere else, one can sue someone for doing a
wrong, but not for a failure to act. An exception to this rule already
exists, as we shall see, when there is a special relationship between the
person who was wronged and the person who ought to bear a measure
of responsibility for that wrong. Now I think it is time for another breakthrough in law.

In today's impersonal society, it seems that we simply must create
a new responsibility for wrongs that were formerly left solely to the dictates of conscience.

At the moment, . . . the lawbooks abound with cases that shock
our conscience but hold no one responsible. For example, a child is drowning in a lake. An excellent swimmer passes by and observes the impending
tragedy. He does not choose to go to the rescue, and the child dies. Is
he liable? No. The law imposes no duty upon a stranger to rescue another. Indeed, even if there were a rowboat available for easy use, a life
preserver that could be thrown, a witness could not be taken into court
for failing to use them.

Time and again, doctors who refuse to answer an urgent call of a
sick man in distress have been absolved from liability for the consequences. A layman who sees another bleeding to death and neither applies a tourniquet nor even summons help also cannot be held accountable
to the victim. Since traditional law has assigned him no legal duty, he
is immune from punishment except by the pangs of his own conscience.

The same rule applies to those who fail to warn a child playing on railroad tracks of an approaching train, and to those who do not utter a sound as a worker walks into the jaws of a dangerous machine.

\*    \*    \*    \*    \*

Why has the law been so cautious, through the centuries, in shielding those who do nothing to aid another in distress? The theory has been that someone who by his actions creates a dangerous situation should be responsible, because it is his deed that puts the victim in peril. But the same theory holds that when someone fails to act, he has not made the situation worse; he has not added a mite to the dilemma of the person in trouble. He has merely failed to volunteer the benefit of his interference. Why should he bear a responsibility no one else has, simply because he happens to be on the scene? This is the reason for the present rule. The time has come to reexamine it.

It is not unusual for the law to create liability where for centuries there was none. For example, in times past, assault and battery could be committed only by physical violence. The law did not recognize that words could injure people. Finally the courts conceded that the hurt to a person's sensibilities, when lies were told about him, could be worse than a blackened eye or a broken nose. And so the law of libel was born.

There have been similar breakthroughs in other branches of law when public need demanded a change. For example, it is now the rule of the sea, under maritime law, that it *is* the duty of a ship to go to the rescue of a foundering vessel.

Even where such exceptions have not been formally spelled out, the law has extended the responsibility for failure to act. This responsibility is now limited to those instances where a special relationship exists between the victim and the person who was on the spot when he was wronged. In fact, in such cases, the law carries responsibility even one step farther. For example, if your chauffeur, in the course of his duties, runs over a pedestrian, you are liable although you were sitting at home oblivious to what was going on. The employer-employee relationship creates this responsibility to the victim. A railroad or bus company owes a similar duty to a passenger in peril because of the carrier-passenger relationship; and if a child fell overboard, the boat's owners would be liable if their employees failed to act to save the child. The owners are responsible because of the ship-traveler relationship.

The law extends responsibility for failure to act in such cases under the theory that an *implied* contract exists and creates such a duty. . . .

By the same token, if a citizen tries to save a drowning boy and then unaccountably abandons him, he is liable. Someone who volunteers to take care of a smallpox patient and then lets him escape is even legally responsible to a third person who happens to contract the disease. If you invite a hitchhiker to ride in your automobile, you are responsible to him if he is injured by your negligence. And a doctor who stops on the road to aid an injured man is liable to him if he is guilty of gross negligence in his treatment.

The question is whether we should further extend this extension of the law and make it a citizen's duty to go to the aid of another in distress, *even when there is no special relationship.*

In North Carolina, mere knowledge of serious peril that threatens death or bodily harm to someone else places the duty upon any observing citizen to go to the rescue, as long as he can do so without undue risk. So, for example, a child was knocked off a railroad trestle and fell forty feet, breaking his thigh. He was ignored by a railroad guard and died from exposure during the cold night. The railroad was held responsible in damages for his death. One of our federal courts adopted a similar rule in a maritime case. A ship's captain failed to give aid to a stranger adrift in a small boat. The man sued for damages due to injuries suffered from exposure. The court, citing the International Salvage Treaty, ruled in his favor.

If other states adopt similar laws, they are also very likely to limit a citizen's obligation to help. No witness can be expected to place himself in great danger. The new law would require him to make a simple phone call to the police, but it could not expect martyrdom.

When thugs with guns or knives are belaboring a victim, it is too much to expect an unarmed passerby to hurl himself into the fray. In fact, nowadays such zealous Samaritans had best curb their good intentions. When Ernest Matthews, 21 years old, was recently on his way to his job in a garage, he came upon five men with knives attacking two women and a man. It was 4:30 in the morning. Perhaps he had read the indignant stories about apathetic citizens. In any event, he interfered boldly. It was a disastrous decision: he was stabbed eight times and killed.

Certainly, I do not propose that we adopt a legal standard that requires a citizen to forfeit his life against criminal odds. Only police, armed and trained to cope with such emergencies and sworn to take such risks, are required to be heroic. But surely a citizen must call for help. About 20 citizens were at their windows and watched the attack that caused Ernest Matthews' tragic death. Should they not have been required to sound an alarm?

\*     \*     \*     \*     \*

We cannot delay until the roots of increasing crime . . . are unearthed and torn out. The time has come to require of every citizen a higher standard of preventive conduct than the law has heretofore recognized.

In some foreign countries, such laws are already on the books. In France, the failure of a citizen to act under certain circumstances is deemed a crime. In 1945, the French Penal Code was amended so that anyone who is able to prevent by his immediate action, without risk to himself or to third parties, an act that causes bodily harm to a person, must do so. If he doesn't, he will be punished by one month to three years of imprisonment or a fine of 12,000 to 500,000 francs, or both.

Italy has a similar penal provision. It provides that anybody who finds an abandoned or misplaced child under ten years of age, or a person incapable of providing for himself because of sickness of mind or body or old age, and fails to inform the authorities immediately, may be punished by imprisonment up to three months or fined up to 3,000 lire. If the injury is increased because of inaction, the penalty increases. If death results, the penalty is doubled.

The rule of the Good Samaritan must be formulated into a reasonable legal obligation. The basic philosophy to justify such a breakthrough in law is not new. Voltaire said it long ago: "We must not be guilty of the good things we didn't do."

---

**What Do You Think?**

1. Many people argue that capital punishment does not act as a deterrent to murders. Similarly, do you believe that the sort of legislation proposed by Mr. Nizer would lead citizens to behave more responsibly toward their neighbors? Give reasons to support your answer.

2. When *is* silence a crime? When is it *not* a crime? Explain your thinking.

## 2.  CAN PARENTS HELP? *

*What can parents and other concerned adults do to equip young people to come to grips with alienation? The following advice to parents offers a survey of the root causes of alienation and some cues on how to counteract it.*

The first requirement is a conscious, critical attempt to clarify our personal values and renew our commitment to them. Clearly these values must be concerned with more than earning a living or succeeding in a career. They must include clear concepts of what people and society can and should be. Humanistic values must be part of our idea of the good life, for it is their lack that young people deplore most.

---

* Excerpted from Elizabeth and Dale Harris, "Roots of Alienation," *The PTA Magazine,* May 1968.

No parent need refrain from affirming his values for fear they will not be suited to the world in which his children live. Better to have clear-cut patterns that youth can challenge than fuzzy ones they cannot react to. Alienated youth appear not to have had parental examples of commitment.

Emphasize the significance of values in themselves. Avoid presenting as values mere instruments for reaching goals. Money, for example, is a useful social tool, not a value in itself. Integrity is intrinsically good, not just an expedient front to win power or public office. When compromises must be made, show what is being preserved by the compromise. If we move more slowly toward social justice than we wish, make plain that we preserve a firmer foundation for justice than if it were won by violence.

Help children to like and respect themselves. For this, acceptance and warmth, consideration of one's wants as a person, and a definite place in the family are fundamental. The delinquent, the violent, and the most hopeless and bitter have not had these security-giving experiences. Here we need social action, for adults lacking education and employment are severely limited in the security they can provide for children.

Help children set realistic goals for themselves. In play and in school-work they need goals that they can achieve but that require effort. Help children find satisfaction in effort by celebrating their success.

Then move on toward new objectives without constant praise of past achievements.

Keep communication lines open. While this is especially important during adolescence, parents must start in a child's early years by listening to him as well as by instructing him. Listening to a child, even helping him express his view more adequately, gives him the feeling he is being treated as an individual. This doesn't mean his opinion must prevail. But hearing his view is essential in helping him to understand why he cannot always have his way, and to accept the denial as just and fair.

Spend some time with your children. Join in their interests in a supportive, mature manner, and include them in adult activities when suitable. Don't try to be a child with your child; you will only succeed in being ridiculous. But your child needs to feel your genuine interest in his affairs and to know he can talk to you about them. If he has your respectful interest during his childhood, he will be less likely to shut you out entirely in adolescence.

This point is especially pertinent for fathers. Many, preoccupied with their jobs, keep thinking that shortly they'll find more time for their children. Not a great deal of time is required. An occasional afternoon given to a child on his terms is a good investment for the future as well as fun in the present.

Cultivate an interest in learning, in recreation, and in the arts. Communicate a positive attitude toward learning and continue to learn, for education is the greatest assurance of adaptability.

Express your concern with public matters. Let your child know that you have telephoned a political candidate or written your representative in Congress or worked on a PTA committee. Don't say, "There's nothing I can do." If your child hears only cynical despair about the lot of the individual in mass society, he is not likely to work at preserving his democratic freedom.

Be alert to social change. Think about how changes will benefit or hurt others as well as yourself. Reflect on the changes your parents faced. When the changes hurt, as they may, muster as much humor as you can. Admittedly it is not easy to deal with the experiences and social conditions that produce alienation. But to the extent that a parent commits himself optimistically, generously, and courageously to doing his best for a better world, he insures himself and his children against the devastation of aloneness and emptiness.

---

**What Do You Think?**

Which of the suggestions listed above seem most feasible to you? Why?

### 3. BLACK POWER *

*Since the summer of 1966, the cry for "Black Power" is one that has echoed and re-echoed across the land. In the following reading, two of the leading proponents of Black Power describe its meaning and impact. How is this concept related to alienation?*

Black people in the United States must raise hard questions, questions which challenge the very nature of the society itself: its long-standing values, beliefs and institutions.

To do this, we must first redefine ourselves. Our basic need is to reclaim our history and our identity from what must be called cultural terrorism, from the depredation of self-justifying white guilt. We shall have to struggle for the right to create our own terms through which to define ourselves and our relationship to the society, and to have these

---

* Excerpted from Stokely Carmichael and Charles V. Hamilton, *Black Power: The Politics of Liberation in America,* New York, N. Y.: Random House, Inc., 1967. Copyright © 1967 by Stokely Carmichael and Charles V. Hamilton. Reprinted by permission of Random House, Inc.

terms recognized. This is the first necessity of a free people, and the first right that any oppressor must suspend.

*    *    *    *    *

Black people must redefine themselves, and only *they* can do that. Throughout this country, vast segments of the black communities are beginning to recognize the need to assert their own definitions, to reclaim their history, their culture; to create their own sense of community and togetherness. There is a growing resentment of the word "Negro," for example, because this term is the invention of our oppressor; it is *his* image of us that he describes. Many blacks are now calling themselves African-Americans, Afro-Americans or black people because that is *our* image of ourselves. When we begin to define our own image, the stereotypes—that is, lies—that our oppressor has developed will begin in the white community and end there. The black community will have a positive image of itself that *it* has created. This means we will no longer call ourselves lazy, apathetic, dumb, good-timers, shiftless, etc. Those are words used by white America to define us. If we accept these adjectives, as some of us have in the past, then we see ourselves only in a negative way, precisely the way white America wants us to see ourselves. Our incentive is broken and our will to fight is surrendered. From now on we shall view ourselves as African-Americans and as black people who are in fact energetic, determined, intelligent, beautiful and peace-loving.

There is a terminology and ethos peculiar to the black community of which black people are beginning to be no longer ashamed. Black communities are the only large segments of this society where people refer to each other as brother—soul-brother, soul-sister. Some people may look upon this as *ersatz,* as make-believe, but it is not that. It is real. It is a growing sense of community. It is a growing realization that black Americans have a common bond not only among themselves, but with their African brothers. . . .

More and more black Americans are developing this feeling. They are becoming aware that they have a history which pre-dates their forced introduction to this country. African-American history means a long history beginning on the continent of Africa, a history not taught in the standard textbooks of this country. It is absolutely essential that black people know this history, that they know their roots, that they develop an awareness of their cultural heritage. Too long have they been kept in submission by being told that they had no culture, no manifest heritage, before they landed on the slave auction blocks in this country. If black people are to know themselves as a vibrant, valiant people, they must know their roots. And they will soon learn that the Hollywood image of man-eating cannibals waiting for, and waiting on, the Great White Hunter is a lie.

*    *    *    *    *

Only when black people fully develop this sense of community, of themselves, can they begin to deal effectively with the problems of racism in *this* country. This is what we mean by a new consciousness; this is the vital first step.

The next step is what we shall call the process of political modern-ization—a process which must take place if the society is to be rid of racism. "Political modernization" includes many things, but we mean by it three major concepts: (1) questioning old values and institutions of the society; (2) searching for new and different forms of political struc-ture to solve political and economic problems; and (3) broadening the base of political participation to include more people in the decision-making process. These notions (we shall take up each in turn) are central to our thinking throughout this book and to contemporary American history as a whole. . . .

The values of this society support a racist system; we find it incon-gruous to ask black people to adopt and support most of those values. We also reject the assumption that the basic institutions of this society must be preserved. The goal of black people must *not* be to assimilate into middle-class America, for that class—as a whole—is without a viable conscience as regards humanity. The values of the middle class permit the perpetuation of the ravages of the black community. The values of that class are based on material aggrandizement, not the expansion of humanity. The values of that class ultimately support cloistered little closed societies tucked away neatly in tree-lined suburbia. The values of that class do *not* lead to the creation of an open society. That class *mouths* its preference for a free, competitive society, while at the same time forcefully and even viciously denying to black people as a group the opportunity to compete.

\*     \*     \*     \*     \*

This same middle class manifests a sense of superior group position in regard to race. This class wants "good government" *for themselves;* it wants good schools *for its children.* At the same time, many of its mem-bers sneak into the black community by day, exploit it, and take the money home to their middle-class communities at night to support their operas and art galleries and comfortable homes. When not actually robbing, they will fight off the handful of more affluent black people who seek to move in; when they approve or even seek token integration, it applies only to black people like themselves—as "white" as possible. *This class is the backbone of institutional racism in this country.*

Thus we reject the goal of assimilation into middle-class America because the values of that class are in themselves anti-humanist and be-cause that class as a social force perpetuates racism. We must face the fact that, in the past, what we have called the movement has not really ques-tioned the middle-class values and institutions of this country. If anything, it has accepted those values and institutions without fully realizing their racist nature. Reorientation means an emphasis on the dignity of man, not on the sanctity of property. It means the creation of a society where human misery and poverty are repugnant to that society, not an indication of laziness or lack of initiative. . . .

Black people have seen the city planning commissions, the urban renewal commissions, the boards of education and the police departments fail to speak to their needs in a meaningful way. We must devise new structures, new institutions to replace those forms or to make them responsive. There is nothing sacred or inevitable about old institutions; the focus must be on people, not forms.

Existing structures and established ways of doing things have a way of perpetuating themselves and for this reason, the modernizing process will be difficult. Therefore, timidity in calling into question the boards of education or the police departments will not do. They must be challenged forcefully and clearly. If this means the creation of parallel community institutions, then that must be the solution. If this means that black parents must gain control over the operation of the schools in the black community, then that must be the solution. The search for new forms means the search for institutions that will, for once, make decisions in the interest of black people. It means, for example, a building inspection department that neither winks at violations of building codes by absentee slumlords nor imposes meaningless fines which permit them to continue their exploitation of the black community.

Essential to the modernization of structures is a broadened base of political participation. More and more people must become politically sensitive and active (we have already seen this happening in some areas of the South). People must no longer be tied, by small incentives or handouts, to a corrupting and corruptible white machine. Black people will choose their own leaders and hold those leaders responsible to *them*. . . . Broadening the base of political participation, then, has as much to do with the quality of black participation as with the quantity. We are fully aware that the black vote, especially in the North, has been pulled out of white pockets and "delivered" whenever it was in the interest of white politicians to do so. That vote must no longer be controllable by those who have neither the interests nor the demonstrated concern of black people in mind.

As the base broadens, as more and more black people become activated, they will perceive more clearly the special disadvantages heaped upon them as a group. They will perceive that the larger society is growing more affluent while the black society is retrogressing, as daily life and mounting statistics clearly show. . . . Black people will become increasingly active as they notice that their retrogressive status exists in large measure because of values and institutions arraigned against them. They will begin to stress and strain and call the entire system into question. Political modernization will be in motion. We believe that it is now in motion. One form of that motion is Black Power.

The adoption of the concept of Black Power is one of the most legitimate and healthy developments in American politics and race relations in our time. The concept of Black Power speaks to all the needs mentioned in this chapter. It is a call for black people in this country to unite, to recognize their heritage, to build a sense of community. It is a call for black people to begin to define their own goals, to lead their own organizations and to support those organizations. It is a call to reject the racist institutions and values of this society.

The concept of Black Power rests on a fundamental premise: *Before a group can enter the open society, it must first close ranks.* By this we mean that group solidarity is necessary before a group can operate effectively from a bargaining position of strength in a pluralistic society. Traditionally, each new ethnic group in this society has found the route to social and political viability through the organization of its own institutions with which to represent its needs within the larger society. Studies in voting behavior specifically, and political behavior generally, have made it clear that politically the American pot has not melted. Italians vote for Rubino over O'Brien: Irish for Murphy over Goldberg, etc. This phenomenon may seem distasteful to some, but it has been and remains today a central fact of the American political system.

\*       \*       \*       \*       \*

The point is obvious: black people must lead and run their own organizations. Only black people can convey the revolutionary idea—and it is a revolutionary idea—that black people are able to do things themselves. Only they can help create in the community an aroused and continuing black consciousness that will provide the basis for political strength. In the past, white allies have often furthered white supremacy without the whites involved realizing it, or even wanting to do so. Black people must come together and do things for themselves. They must achieve self-identity and self-determination in order to have their daily needs met.

Black Power means, for example, that in Lowndes County, Alabama, a black sheriff can end police brutality. A black tax assessor and tax collector and county board of revenue can lay, collect, and channel tax monies for the building of better roads and schools serving black people. In such areas as Lowndes, where black people have a majority, they will attempt to use power to exercise control. This is what they seek: control. When black people lack a majority, Black Power means proper representation and sharing of control. It means the creation of power bases, of strength, from which black people can press to change local or nationwide patterns of oppression—instead of from weakness.

It does not mean *merely* putting black faces into office. Black visibility is not Black Power. Most of the black politicians around the country today are not examples of Black Power. The power must be that of a community, and emanate from there. The black politicians must start from there. The black politicians must stop being representatives of "downtown" machines, whatever the cost might be in terms of lost patronage and holiday handouts.

Black Power recognizes—it must recognize—the ethnic basis of American politics as well as the power-oriented nature of American politics. Black Power therefore calls for black people to consolidate behind their own, so that they can bargain from a position of strength. But while we endorse the *procedure* of group solidarity and identity for the purpose of attaining certain goals in the body politic, this does not mean that black people should strive for the same kind of rewards (i.e., end results) obtained by the white society. The ultimate values and goals are not domination or exploitation of other groups, but rather an effective share in the total power of the society.

---

**What Do You Think?**

> Compare Carmichael's and Hamilton's attitudes with those expressed by Louis Nizer in Reading 1. What are the differences? Similarities? How would you explain these differences and similarities?

## 4.   A FEW RAYS OF HOPE *

*In the previous reading the authors urge black people to embrace the Black Power concept as a way of combatting the white Establishment and their own sense of alienation. The following reading describes a cooperative project of government, business, and private citizens to help the ghetto hard-core unemployed help themselves. Which approach offers more hope? Is a compromise possible?*

Diseased debris rotting under a halo of mosquitoes in a vacant lot. Teen-age girls ducking and punching with the fluent fury of grown men. Vomit staining the gutter. Burned-out houses with families living behind the boarded-up windows. Bedford-Stuyvesant's everyday reality is filled with the surreal imagery of a bad LSD trip. . . .

---

* Excerpted from Jack Newfield, "A Few Rays of Hope," *Life* Magazine, March 8, 1968, © 1968 Time, Inc.

Then, the statistics: Eighty per cent of the teen-agers high school dropouts. Thirty-six per cent of the families headed by women. Twenty-seven per cent with annual incomes under $3,000. The highest infant mortality rate in the country. One of the highest homicide rates in the country. And no one has ever counted the rats. . . .

An earnest and direct attempt to combat [the ghetto] sense of worth-lessness began last June 24, with the announcement of a $7 million grant from the Labor Department to finance a radical new bipartisan project that would try to regenerate Bedford-Stuyvesant. . . .

Simply put, the project is a holistic, systematic attack on urban poverty starting with the idea of convincing private enterprise to invest massively in the ghetto. . . .

The plan is for big business to create jobs by bringing in franchises for national chains, by setting up industrial plants, shopping centers and office buildings. Interrelated are government-subsidized programs to train residents for jobs, to rebuild housing, improve health and educational facilities. Linked up, too, is the idea of generating a new sense of com-munity, and there are showpiece projects such as an athletic and cultural complex, a community college . . . and two super blocks—dead-end streets where grassy malls and playgrounds will replace gutters and rubble. The broad hope is to move along without promising instant upheaval and to hope for a continual crescendo with participation building person by person, street by street, after each accomplishment.

From conservatives the project borrows a faith in private enterprise to function with more technical know-how and less bureaucracy than the federal government. From the New Left it borrows the Black Power concept of helping Negroes gain a sense of pride, participation and community by giving them control of decisions. From the current Ad-ministration it accepts the New Deal premise that federal government has a responsibility to subsidize efforts to help the bottom third of society. It has turned the nation's biggest ghetto into its biggest laboratory.

Two nonprofit corporations have been set up. One—called the Bed-ford-Stuyvesant Restoration Corporation—consists of about 25 grass-roots community leaders and is responsible for creating and implementing training programs, employment opportunities, community development programs. A temporary headquarters has been established at the Hotel Granada, on the edge of Bedford-Stuyvesant. . . . At the Granada the faces, from the secretaries on up, are black. And even the revolutionaries from CORE feel at home.

The second corporation is named D&S (Development and Services) whose purpose is to raise funds, generate ideas, bring in the new busi-ness and provide the community with technical expertise in administration. "But all the major decisions, . . . will be made by the commu-nity."

Based on its idealized blueprints, the Bedford-Stuyvesant program could become a national model for slum regeneration. . . .

For its first effort the Restoration Corporation chose to renovate the exteriors of more than 400 four-story houses in an 11-block area. When fixed up, the buildings would be highly visible symbols, proof to the community that something could be accomplished. Also the renovation would immediately create jobs for 272 unemployed, unskilled residents, who would be trained and paid $1.70 an hour to do the work. "We call this a multiple-impact program," says a director. "You reach the unemployed, teach them skills and improve the community."

Last July teams of Restoration canvassers fanned out, asking residents merely to sign up, pay a token fee of $25 for renovation work valued at $325 and agree to sweep their sidewalks and maintain at least two garbage cans. Modesto Bravo, president of the Halsey Street Block Association, was shocked at how difficult it was to enlist his neighbors. "I went from house to house," he says, "but they didn't want to cooperate. They just didn't believe it."

The ghetto's cynicism had congealed so hard everyone suspected the renovation offer was a hustle, or a gimmick. Bravo could not get a dialogue going. Finally, he obtained some police barricades and held a street meeting. "Passers-by stopped out of curiosity and started to ask questions," he says, "and it started to boom. In the end 98 per cent signed up."

But then there were problems with the trainees. The Restoration staff had to walk the streets recruiting and convincing people that no questions would be asked about criminal records or narcotics contact. They expected to attract only youngsters but ended up with a group averaging 22–24 years, including some over 40. For many, it was the first full-time job after working sporadically as dishwashers or messengers.

Absenteeism was 25 per cent. "You have to start from the beginning and teach them what demands work makes under real circumstances," says Thomas. "You have to teach them to show up regularly, to be on time, that work makes demands on one's time."

Confidence lagged. "If a kid was told he was going to be trained how to rig a scaffold, or cement a sidewalk," says Thomas, "his first reaction was that he'd never learn how to do it. They lacked a base of confidence." Thomas' aide, Jim Lowry, says, "They can see the possibilities on the horizon, but they can't believe it's for them. Too much has happened to them by the time we reach them." . . .

Thomas and his staff persisted—pushing, coaxing, teaching, understanding. The 272 trainees they finally signed up learned skills from 34 instructors who had previously been unemployed or underemployed themselves. Then they plastered stoops, fixed sidewalks, painted doors. They installed railings, pruned trees, sodded backyards. They were taught carpentry, ironwork, gardening, painting. . . .

By September, Halsey Street was renovated, and the residents celebrated at a block party, then, on their own, collected money for trees to improve the street further. Three of the trainees and two of their training officers formed their own firm, visited the homes they had helped restore and asked if there now was any work they could do on the interiors. Presently, they contracted to repair kitchens, patch up ceilings, fix floors, paint walls. The trainees' gardening instructor also set up his own company and hired his trainees.

In all, Restoration was able to send back to school or find work for 225 of the trainees from the renovation project. Eighty more unskilled, unemployed people from the community were put to work conducting a survey of what, exactly, their neighbors wanted done in the community. Many of these canvassers are now being trained in analyzing data methods and in basic concepts of city planning. Eventually they will be stationed in three renovated storefronts as community advisers, helping residents through such bureaucratic struggles as the filing of city housing complaints. More local people have begun demolishing the abandoned milk bottling plant. On the site a community complex will soon rise, housing meeting rooms for residents, office space for city service organizations and day-care centers for children. The blueprints have been drawn up by Negro architects, and construction, says a Restoration official, will be done by local contractors "even if they have not done work on this scale before."

Progress has been significant—psychologically encouraging, a foundation for the future, broad in scope though lean in actual inroads. It is a vicious cycle the Restoration staff faces, breaking through the layers of protective skepticism, getting the bitter and the poor motivated, then running up against massive institutional barriers like union bigotry or limited funds, and, as a result of that, having to deal all over again with the original cynicism and despair. . . .

The future, as always is inscrutable. Riot smoke rises from "model cities" like Detroit and New Haven no less than it rises from rotting, backward cities like Newark and Buffalo. A riot, a scandal, a political rupture can still hurt the Bedford-Stuyvesant experiment. Yet walking through the community, one senses something—if not yet the beginning of optimism, then at least the end of impotence.

---

**What Do You Think?**

What advantages does this approach to dealing with alienation have over some of the other approaches you have read about? Disadvantages?

## 5.   A PIECE OF THE ACTION *

*This next reading suggests that the students need to know that adults "really care." What is the connection between caring and alienation?*

His friends called him J.P. He was a popular boy, despite his obvious lack of interest in what was happening in the classrooms. He had a quick smile and a ready sense of humor. Everyone thought of him as being "sharp"—but his grades were terrible. His teachers had generally given up on him long ago, and little by little his smile faded and his wisecracks became fewer and feebler. Eventually, he didn't say much of anything to anyone, and then, one day, he wasn't there anymore.

James P. Morgan had gotten the message: There wasn't anything in school for him. He became dropout number 743 from the District of Columbia school system in January of last year. . . .

It's very likely that J.P. could have been kept in school if we had taken the trouble to find something he really wanted to know about. Obviously he wasn't stupid; he wasn't even particularly lazy. He was just a stranger in a strange world, looking for something friendly and comfortable to hang on to—some sign of success.

On the other hand, there's young Jefferson Barnes. . . . He spent 10 minutes with me and told me more than most people ever get to hear about the right way to handle what we have come to call the "alienated youth problem" in our high schools.

Jeff had been a lot like J.P. at one point—ready to drop out or be squeezed out, depending on how you look at it. But he was lucky. By the time he got to that point, there was a program waiting for him.

In the months between the time Jeff graduated from high school and the time he joined the Marines, he held one job in the daytime as a bank teller and another in the evening as a part-time bookkeeper for an auto dealer. He had set aside enough money to get married and start a savings account. His voice and manner reflected the enthusiasm and confidence he felt about his future plans.

Jeff expects to get enough post-secondary education when he finishes his tour with the Marines so that he can fit into a well-paying job in the computer field, perhaps as a programer. He's sure he can do it, and I think so, too.

What was the big difference between J.P. and Jeff? There was none.

---

* Excerpted from Leon P. Minear, "A Piece of the Action," *American Education,* March 1969.

They were both the same type of student. The difference was in what happened to them.

No one noticed J.P. until it was too late. Mrs. Thorpe noticed Jeff, got his attention, and enrolled him in a cooperative education program that made sense to him. The program sent him out into the working world as a responsible, well-motivated young man. That was the difference.

People have been talking about alienated youth as if there is something wrong with these youngsters. They rarely think about the possibility that the problem may lie with society itself, a society which has failed in many, many cases to provide an understandable role for the young person to fit himself into, a society which no longer has many options left to offer youth.

One of the great American tragedies in the past two decades has been the almost total isolation of young people from an effective role in society, a role with dignity and value.

In some ways, public schools have functioned as a mechanism for keeping many students—rich and poor, black and white, bright and slow —uninvolved in the serious activities of our society. . . .

One of the most vivid manifestations of this problem of alienation is rebellion. Surprisingly, it is not rebellion against authority so much as rebellion for a greater piece of the action. Young people want *in,* and schools must find ways to let them in.

This may mean making it possible for one student to earn enough money while in school to buy a secondhand car. It may mean making it possible for another to get deeply involved in some sort of social action. Whatever the particulars, it is clear that young people are telling the schools to make learning mean something tangible and to give them opportunities to make direct contributions to society. It is up to the schools to meet these demands.

The school systems, especially in their vocational programs and through their vocational teachers, have the tools and the plans to get young people involved in adult activities.

What is the major adult activity? Work. And the work role is open to us as educators to help young people find their piece of the action— not just the drudgery of work, but the experience of work; the knowledge that comes from and the responsibility that goes with earning while learning; the feeling of being a significant part of society.

---

**What Do You Think?**

The author suggests that students need a "piece of the action." What does he mean? Would you agree? Why or why not?

### 6.   A BILL OF RIGHTS FOR KIDS *

*One approach to the alienation of our young people might be to clarify the bases of parent-child and school-student relationships. The next selection attempts to outline a framework within which that might be accomplished.*

The American Bill of Rights sets forth inalienable rights of its citizens —adults, that is. In addition, grown-ups—and surely parents and teachers—claim unto themselves hundreds of privileges and rights, not all of them commendable.

But what about our non-adults . . . our non-citizens, our children? What rights do they have? Not many, I am afraid. . . . "Shut up and do as you are told," is often an answer. So I suggest "A Bill of Rights for Kids," at least in our adult minds, which might even include the right of children on occasion to "talk back" when unfairly treated and to refuse to obey some of our silly and senseless commands. . . .

Among the more serious rights I believe children should have are these:

*The right to be understood.* Children cry out, inwardly and outwardly, for adults to see their points of view once in awhile. They plead that we will hold off our answer or our decisions at least long enough to listen to their explanation. They usually have reasons—and many times good reasons—for what they say and do.

*The right to question—and to know.* All children are born with a curiosity and a desire to learn. These precious attributes are often blunted when their quest for knowledge is answered by "I don't have time now," "Go ask someone else," "That's a silly question," or "Go look it up." What's worse, we make fun of many of their attempts to learn, and quash their enthusiasms and attempts with low grades, failure, rebukes and punishment. We almost dare them to keep on asking.

*The right to be different.* Somehow, we adults keep ignoring the truth that children are different, and that one of the wonderful aspects of the human race is that each individual is unique. We expect kids to be alike, we give them the same tasks, judge them with the same tests, and treat them the same. "Be like your older brother," we parents often urge, especially if older brother has been a star.

*The right to learn successfully.* No greater motivation is needed for any of us to do a job than that of success. For children, this means the

---

* Excerpted from Marshall C. Jameson, "A Bill of Rights for Kids."

right to be allowed to learn and to solve problems which are within the great possibility of success, not above or below where success can be achieved. If we will listen, we will hear our children asking, "Please do not force me into areas of learning which I am not yet prepared to handle." If we heed their pleading, we will stop timing learning, failing kids, and setting unreal standards.

*The right to be a child.* In these times, adulthood is being forced down upon our children more and more, making our kids really small adults. Society has thought it cute to have children be like, dress like, act like grown-ups. We force adult social customs and activities upon them (a formal party, with corsages, at age eleven), and constantly scream at them, "Act like a little gentleman!" One child did talk back saying to his parents, "I ain't done being a kid, yet."

*The right to some private thought of their own.* Would adults like it if some authority over us could make us spill out at request every thought we had in our minds—force us to answer truthfully any question asked of us? Yet this is exactly what we do as parents and teachers, forcing children to "come clean" regardless of what is asked. "Now, tell the truth," we command, and often force our children to fib in order for them to maintain even a bit of self-esteem. Children ought to have the right, too, to daydream—and keep it secret.

Being a child must be a very difficult thing these days. Adults have forgotten just what it is like to be a child—and to have so few rights. Perhaps parents and teachers, with the children helping us, could actually write down some rights that they really should have, and then honor this new document.

---

**What Do You Think?**

1. Mr. Jameson indicates that he believes his list of rights contains some of the "more serious" rights. Do you agree or not? Would you add or omit any from the list? Explain.

2. Some people would say that the proposal of the writer is so superficial as to be meaningless. How do you react to that charge? Explain.

3. What suggestions might you make for dealing with the problems of the alienation of young people in America?

## 7. I CARE, YOU CARE, HE CARES

*Here is an example of how one individual combatted alienation in prison. What does his action suggest for those of us outside of prison?*

Recently I read an article by Arthur Gordon about "Caring" which jarred me out of my usual lethargy with the message: "The more things you care about, the more intensely you care, the more alive you become."

At first I thought this message applied to the man on the streets. Every time I enter the front gates of a prison I tuck all of my caring away in a place where I store my "street habits." Still, the article disturbed me. Later that evening when the dormitory had settled down to the coughs and muffled groans of men either asleep or fighting to get to sleep, I remembered an incident which happened years ago, in another penitentiary.

I was sitting beside No. 1 building on a scorching California summer day. The shade from the building extended two or three feet from the benches and offered a limited refuge. Cherokee, Scotty, and I lounged in droopy-eyed discomfort while we watched another con come down from the upper yard. As he passed us, he made an obscene remark about the heat. We heard him clearly, and ignored him.

Two other men who were seated up the bench from us must have heard only the last part of what he said. They immediately stiffened, their dull conversation stopped by the tightening of their mouths. Moon, a full-blooded Zuni with a complete understanding of curse words, jumped up and ran to a rack where a punching bag hung limp, and reached on top for a pick handle he had stashed there. His partner, Pat, a homosexual turned wolf after the flush of youth had worn off, drew a length of two-inch pipe from under the bench.

The other convicts sitting silently and watching with me—we knew from the beginning what the misunderstanding was all about. We knew the attackers and we knew what was going to happen. Still, we waited in salty-mouthed anticipation; none of us thought to warn the victim. It was hot, and we just did not care. After all, it was not our beef.

The man who had remarked about the miserable heat shuffled on, completely unaware of having offended anyone, until Pat slipped up behind him and scored a home run off the top of his head. Moon's crushing blow in the middle of his back sent him to the ground.

Any man who has done time has seen what the quick flaring vio-

---

* Excerpted from Jim Little, "I Care, You Care, He Cares," *Harper's Magazine,* April 1964. Copyright © 1964, by Harper's Magazine, Inc.

lence of men who do not care can do to men who, because of their utter hopelessness, care even less. Those who have not done time need not be burdened with the details of how a helpless man writhes on the ground and sobs for the mercy of oblivion.

While we were watching the beating in mild amusement, another breed of man came by. He was not a personal friend of the man seeking protection in the bloody dust, nor did he have a vested interest in the welfare of the two grunting attackers. But he stepped between the creature on the ground and the men swinging their lethal weapons. He held up his empty hands to show that he was unarmed. Standing relaxed, he seemed to ignore the victim while he studied the panting men in front of him.

"That's enough," was all he said while he continued to stand relaxed, quiet, watching.

Moon, the bully boy with the pick handle, made a threatening gesture. He said, "Man, you buying into this?" The passer-by shrugged a non-committal answer and continued to stand quietly. He seemed to look through Moon and Pat until they turned and threw their weapons down.

Cherokee, Scotty, and I looked away. The salty taste in my mouth had turned metallic, dry. We avoided each other's eyes when the passer-by kneeled down to help the injured man. One man got up then and helped escort the victim across the big yard toward the hospital. The rest of us shifted around in silent discomfort while we died a little more inside. I wish I could say it was me who got up to help, but it wasn't.

Remembering all this did not miraculously make me begin caring about anyone or anything, though it did take a little of the curl out of my lip. I am still not sure this isolated incident proves that the article was right, that "The more things you care about, and the more intensely you care, the more alive you become." But it does seem to indicate that the fewer things you care about, the more indifferent you become, the "deader" you are.

The few times I have taken a "calculated" risk by deliberately discarding my shell of indifference, I have felt rich inside. A guy with enough practice might develop a meaningful way to live in prison. Who knows? This caring-bit might be the first step toward a more purposeful life on the streets.

---

**What Do You Think?**

What does the author mean when he states "this caring-bit might be the first step toward a more purposeful life on the streets"? How would you define caring? Is caring, as you define it, one way to deal with alienation? Explain.

### 8.   COLUMBIA—THE NEXT AMERICA? *

*One way of combatting the alienating conditions of our large metro-
politan areas is to attempt to deal with each of them directly within
the context of the traditional city. Another way is through the building of "new towns" where the psychological and social needs of the
residents are taken into account before the city appears. The following
article describes one such "new town."*

"Where can you live today with swimming pools, golf courses,
riding stables, tennis clubs, 3,200 acres of green meadows, woods,
lakes, streams, hills forever preserved in their natural beauty, where
the symphony concert is just a few minutes from your door, where
you can swim warm while you see the snow fall, where you can canter
over miles of equestrian trails before breakfast, where you can work
as butcher, baker, candlestick maker, lawyer or industrial chief,
where a speedy little mini-bus whisks you from almost anywhere to
any place else in the city for only a dime, where you can rent, buy
or build an apartment, town house, home or country place, where a
great city's excitement is beginning to happen in the middle of historic estate country, where you can walk your hound in the woods,
or hunt pheasant, quail or duck in a game preserve, where you can
stroll downtown to go sailing, where tomorrow your children will be
educated in the newest schools, junior college and university, where
you can get a pastrami or pumpernickle at two in the morning from
the delicatessen, where shops, theatres, restaurants will bring you the
best the world has to offer, and where you'll live like you earned
$5,000 a year more than you do?"

The multipart question and its mildly prophetic answer . . . (both re-
produced directly from an advertisement which appeared . . . in Baltimore and Washington newspapers) are Columbia's way of announcing
that it is open for business.

Columbia is, of course, the main town that James W. Rouse has
been nurturing, planning, and developing . . . in Howard County, Mary-
land, midway between Baltimore and Washington. Only its first stage
of development . . . is nearing completion. . . .

But it is enough to give cadence to the claims made in the ad (al-
lowing for a certain amount of poetic license) and to provide strong

---

* Excerpted from James Bailey, "Only in Columbia, the Next America," *Archi-
tectural Forum,* November 1967. Copyright 1967 Urban America, Inc.

clues about how Columbia is fulfilling the goals—economic, social, and physical—established for it.

At Columbia, the three goals are being pursued in a unique kind of way that sets it apart from the hundred-odd new towns and so-called "new towns" that are currently in various phases of development in the U. S. . . . Rouse . . . has developed a physical plan that embodies the contribution not only of planners and urban designers, but of experts in such fields as sociology, psychology, government, recreation, economics, education, health, housing, transportation, and communication.

Rouse, a successful mortgage banker and shopping center developer, believes there can be an alternative to what he has called "the vast, formless spread of housing, pierced by the unrelated scattering of schools, churches, and stores" that heretofore has characterized most urban expansion. But he also believes that such an alternative cannot be produced by high ideals and good intentions alone. Hence Columbia's intensive exploration into the needs and wants of people (carried out by a "work group" of experts in the behavioral sciences and other fields), and its attempts to express these findings in planning and design terms. . . .

Many . . . ingredients, according to Morton Hoppenfeld, Columbia's director of planning and design, were derived from the contributions of the 15-member, multidisciplinary work group which was set up specifically because, in Rouse's words, "there is absolutely no dialogue in the U. S. today between the people who have developed knowledge about people— the teachers, the ministers, psychiatrists, sociologists—and the people who are designing and building our cities."

Because of the work group's participation, Hoppenfeld claims, Columbia will be a much different place than it would have been had the planners and designers acted solely from "our own biases" of what a good city should be. "The work group," Hoppenfeld says, "helped us to realize that the institutions and activities which go on at all levels—interpersonal, interfamily, intergroup, etc.—are fundamental to the quality of life, and fundamental in establishing the form of a city. We had a lot of plan ideas, based on inadequate rationales, but the work group gave us a proper frame of reference. We became much more sensitive to the social purpose of planning."

It was the work group's deliberations that led to what Hoppenfeld has called Columbia's "pivotal planning decision": to acknowledge learning as a basic foundation for a human community. In physical terms this meant schools, and at Columbia schools will become the focal point of each level of community life. For each neighborhood (300 to 500 families) there will be an elementary school, and for each village (3,000 to 5,000 families), a secondary school—all of them within easy walking distance of the areas they serve.

"But we knew," Hoppenfeld says, "that schools were not sufficient in themselves and, in thinking through other human needs, we made the schools the hub of a complementary set of other community facilities and services." Thus each neighborhood complex will contain not only an elementary school, but a day care center, a small store with a snack bar, a meeting room (which Hoppenfeld calls a "neighborhood front room"), a swimming pool, a park, and playgrounds. At the village level, the secondary school will be the focal point of the village center, containing a shopping mall, multipurpose community building, public library, swimming pool, tennis club, and other facilities. . . .

Columbia is now laying plans for a downtown cultural center, where persons engaged in all the arts will live and work together in the kind of close interrelationship that is lacking in most urban areas. The center will contain legitimate theaters, movie houses, art galleries, studios and apartments, shops, and other art-related facilities.

### INTERFAITH VENTURES

The same kind of "togetherness" philosophy is being applied to the community's churches. A cooperative ministry, made up of representatives of Protestant, Catholic, and Jewish faiths, has been set up to plan and build the churches and to work up cooperative ventures for serving the religious needs of the citizens. The church group will also sponsor the first middle-income housing project planned for Columbia—a total of 250 units to be scattered in small groups throughout the villages.

These and literally dozens of other social and institutional activities are being pursued at Columbia. And it is within that context, and within the overriding view that a city is a system of interlocking parts, rather than a collection of separate organisms, that the new town's physical form —the planning, architecture, and urban design—are being carried out. . . .

Last month, addressing a group of visiting planners, William E. Finley, Columbia's director of development (and himself a planner), spelled out the criteria that have been set for Columbia:

"To absorb population growth, metropolitan overspill. To preserve portions of the countryside; to set aside land for a wide range of housing types and for commercial, industrial, educational, cultural, institutional development so critical in the achievement of a well-rounded community.

"To set aside permanent open-space land for 'the lungs of the city.' To provide opportunities for new institutions that will better meet human needs than the older established ones.

"To establish communities that provide for a high degree of human communication, for freedom of movement, freedom from fears, freedom from the depressing aspects of the older cities.

"To provide the technical and legal framework which assures continued maintenance of the community. To stand off the forces of blight and assure the prevention of slums.

"To reduce the journey to work. To allow a person to live and work in the same community with sufficient residential and job mobility to allow vocational growth.

"To provide a wide range of community facilities immediately, as needed, not years after, when a whole generation has grown without them." . . .

"To achieve a democratic social balance, to provide a wide range of housing by type, style, and price. Housing open to all. Housing available to every person employed in the community."

To Columbia's planners and designers, these are not just vague ideals to be wished for, but specific goals to be systematically pursued. It will take a lot more time, a lot more buildings, and a lot more people before the answers are known.

Columbia will be a fascinating place to watch over the coming years.

---

**What Do You Think?**

1. Bailey titled his article, "Only in Columbia, the Next America." What does he mean? Do you think that he is right or wrong? Be sure to give reasons for your answers.
2. What kind of America would the "next America" be? In what ways does this new town seem to combat alienation? Or, does it combat alienation? Support your answer.

## 9. PARTICIPATORY DEMOCRACY *

*In this selection, the author comments on the widespread political alienation in this country and offers some suggestions for dealing with the conditions that contribute to that alienation.*

If democracy means that the individual expresses his conviction and asserts his will, the premise is that he has a conviction, and that he has a will. The facts, however, are that the modern, alienated individual has opinions and prejudices but no convictions, has likes and dislikes, but no will. His opinions and prejudices, likes and dislikes, are manipulated in

---

* Excerpted from Erich Fromm, *The Sane Society,* New York, N. Y.: Holt, Rinehart and Winston, 1955. Copyright © 1955 by Erich Fromm. Reprinted by permission of Holt, Rinehart and Winston, Inc.

the same way as his taste is, by powerful propaganda machines—which might not be effective were he not already conditioned to such influences by advertising and by his whole alienated way of life.

The average voter is poorly informed too. While he reads his newspapers regularly, the whole world is so alienated from him that nothing makes real sense or carries real meaning. He reads of billions of dollars being spent, of millions of people being killed; figures, abstractions, which are in no way interpreted in a concrete, meaningful picture of the world. The science fiction he reads is little different from the science news. Everything is unreal, unlimited, impersonal. Facts are so many lists of memory items, like puzzles in a game, not elements on which his life and that of his children depend. It is indeed a sign of resilience and basic sanity of the average human being, that in spite of these conditions, political choices today are not entirely irrational, but that to some extent sober judgment finds expression in the process of voting.

\*     \*     \*     \*     \*

The voter simply expresses preferences between two candidates competing for his vote. He is confronted with various political machines, with a political bureaucracy which is torn between good will for the best for the country, and the professional interest of keeping in office, or getting back into it. This political bureaucracy, needing votes, is, of course, forced to pay attention to the will of the voter to some extent. Any signs of great dissatisfaction force the political parties to change their course in order to obtain votes, and any sign of a very popular course of action will induce them to continue it. . . . But aside from the restricting or furthering influence which the electorate has on the decisions of the political bureaucracy, and which is more an indirect than a direct influence, there is little the individual citizen can do to participate in the decision-making. Once he has cast his vote, he has abdicated his political will to his representative, who exercises it according to the mixture of responsibility and egotistical professional interest which is characteristic of him, and the individual citizen can do little except vote at the next election, which gives him a chance to continue his representative in office or "to throw the rascals out." The voting process in the great democracies has more and more the character of a plebiscite, in which the voter cannot do much more than register agreement or disagreement with powerful political machines, to one of which he surrenders his political will.

The progress of the democratic process from the middle of the nineteenth to the middle of the twentieth centuries is one of the enlargement of franchise, which has by now led to the general acceptance of unrestricted and universal suffrage. But even the fullest franchise is not enough. The further progress of the democratic system must take a new step. In the first place, it must be recognized that true decisions cannot be made in an atmosphere of mass voting, but only in the relatively small groups corresponding perhaps to the old Town Meeting, and comprising not more than let us say five hundred people. In such small groups the issues at stake can be discussed thoroughly, each member can express his ideas, can listen to, and discuss reasonably other arguments. People have personal contact with each other, which makes it more difficult for demagogic and irrational influences to work on their minds. Secondly, the individual citizen must be in the possession of vital facts which enable him to make a reasonable decision. Thirdly, whatever he, as a member of such a small and face-to-face group, decides, must have a direct influence on the decision-making exercised by a centrally elected parliamentary executive. If this were not so, the citizen would remain as politically stupid as he is today.

The question arises whether such a system of combining a centralized form of democracy, as it exists today, with a high degree of decentralization is possible; whether we can reintroduce the principle of the Town Meeting into modern industrialized society.

I do not see any insoluble difficulty in this. One possibility is to organize the whole population into small groups of say five hundred people, according to local residence, or place of work, and as far as possible these groups should have a certain diversification in their social composition. These groups would meet regularly, let us say once a month, and choose their officials and committees, which would have to change every year. Their program would be the discussion of the main political issues, both of local and of national concern. According to the principle mentioned above, any such discussion, if it is to be reasonable, will require a certain amount of factual information. How can this be given? It seems perfectly feasible that a cultural agency, which is politically independent, can exercise the function of preparing and publishing factual data to be used as material in these discussions. This is only what we do in our school system, where our children are given information which is relatively objective and free from the influence of fluctuating governments. One could imagine arrangements, for instance, by which personalities from the fields of art, sciences, religion, business, politics, whose outstanding achievements and moral integrity are beyond doubt, could be chosen to form a nonpolitical cultural agency. They would differ in their political views, but it can be assumed that they could agree reasonably on what is to be considered objective information about facts. In the case of disagreement, different sets of facts could be presented to the citizens, explaining the basis for the difference. After the small face-to-face groups have received information and have discussed matters, they will vote; with the help of the technical devices we have today, it would be very easy to register the over-all result of these votes in a short time, and the problem would be how decisions arrived at in this way could be channeled into the level of the central government and made effective in the field of decision-making. There is no reason why forms for this process could not be found. In the parliamentary tradition we have usually two parliamentary houses, both participating in the decision-making, but elected according to different principles. The decision of the face-to-face groups would constitute the true "House of Commons," which would share power with the house of universally elected representatives and a universally elected executive. In this way, decision-making would constantly flow, not only from above to below, but from below to above, and it would be based on an active and responsible thinking of the individual citizen. Through the discussion and voting in small face-to-face groups, a good deal of the irrational and abstract character of decision-making would disappear, and political problems would become in reality a concern for the citizen. The process of alienation in which the individual citizen surrenders his political will by the ritual of voting to powers beyond him would be reversed, and each individual would take back into himself his role as a participant in the life of the community.

---

**What Do You Think?**

1.  Some people object to Fromm's proposal on participatory democracy on the grounds that it might lead to a "tyranny of the majority." What does that phrase mean? Do you think that objection is a legitimate one? Why or why not? What other objections might be raised?

2.  Can you apply Fromm's proposal to any of the other alienating situations that you have studied? For example, what relevance do his ideas have for the alienation of young people in America?

## 10.  KILMER: PORTRAIT OF A JOB CORPS CENTER *

*Once a person becomes aware of his own alienation, what can he do to counteract it? The following article describes how the Job Corps helped some young people who took the first step.*

It looks like nowhere—barren, muddy, the white barracks standing in regimental order, forlorn in the winter sun, each marked with its function: *Electrical Construction, Food Service, Welding, Electronics, Read-*

---

* Excerpted from Peter Schrag, *Saturday Review,* March 16, 1968. Copyright 1968 Saturday Review, Inc.

*ing Center, Automotive, Orientation, Counselling.* Four million soldiers passed through here in World War II—there is still a post of Army reserves—and the military aroma was never quite expunged, either from the buildings or the program. But the GI boots are now on other feet, and the action behind the chain link fence is now part of a different war. ANY BOY CAN JOIN THE JOB CORPS, reads the sign behind the gatehouse at the entrance. IT TAKES A *MAN* TO STICK WITH IT.

There are 1,700 of them at Kilmer, some of them boys of twenty-one, others men at sixteen. Three-fourths of them are, as the euphemism goes, "nonwhite," most of them are from Northern cities and all of them are, by virtue of their presence alone, one-time failures—unemployed mountaineers, dropouts from Harlem, semiliterate farm boys from Maine. As a group they are not significantly different from their 40,000 fellow Corpsmen (a fourth of whom are women, who are assigned to separate centers) in the nation's 123 other Job Corps camps. Each man receives $30 a month for personal expenses, plus clothing—a GI outfit, boots, and some formal garb. (Each, on completing a program, also receives $50 for each month enrolled.) Before they joined, 80 per cent had not seen a doctor or a dentist in ten years; 64 per cent had been asked to quit school; 60 per cent are from broken homes. Although all are between sixteen and twenty-one, they have, on the average, completed just over eight years of school and read at a fifth-grade level. Some were thrown out of school for hitting teachers, others just quit. A few have petty criminal records. Many are just the victims of uninterrupted defeat. None-theless, most of them, as a Kilmer teacher said, "are a lot better than they think they are." The very act of joining the Job Corps is a confession of inadequacy, and therefore an act of courage.

What they came for—what Kilmer is supposed to do—is to turn failure into success, into hope and motivation. . . .

"We're in the business of changing attitudes," said William F. Grady, Kilmer's deputy director for program, "and don't let them tell you otherwise." As a consequence, Kilmer and other centers have become examples of one of the most unusual social enterprises ever attempted in America. The Job Corps is an institutional attempt to move society's losers into the middle class. "There's a motto in the Job Corps," the new arrivals are told at an orientation meeting: "to learn, to earn, and to work." Much of the Job Corps, finally, is pure Horatio Alger.

Kilmer, which opened in 1965, is a combination educational institution, trade school, military camp, and counseling center. . . . Kilmer's 600-man staff is such a mixture of backgrounds and styles that it becomes almost impossible to characterize. Company officials, social workers, shop foremen, teachers, retired military officers, psychologists, college students—they're all here, talking not only about reading levels and vocational proficiency, but also about AWOLs, role-playing, review boards, KP, duty officers, sanctions, morale, and operations research. A variety of social and educational techniques are being tried, sometimes in fruitful collaboration, sometimes in a cacophony of demands and instructions that seem to leave at least some Corpsmen with the feeling that, as one of them said, "this is the biggest damn runaround I've ever seen."

Runaround or not, much of it seems to work, not only in job placements but in confidence and maturity. . . .

For the Corpsmen, all of whom live in sixty-four-man dormitories, the day begins at 6 A.M. and ends at 11 P.M., when lights must be out. It includes three hours of academic instruction (usually in classes of ten or twelve), three hours of vocational training, a mandatory "group meeting" in the dormitory, housekeeping chores, and enough free time for basketball in the gymnasium, a few games of pool in the recreation building, and television (where the cartoons are the preferred programs). Most Corpsmen take two academic courses—one in mathematics, the other in "Communications and Social Education," a combination of reading, social studies, and practical information: how to apply for jobs, relocate in a new community, and survive as a consumer. . . .

Much of Kilmer's formal teaching takes place in one-to-one situations, and most of it depends on a subtle mixture of encouragement and candor. (Or perhaps it is all candor when the teachers really believe that their students can learn.) In a mathematics class, a group of Corpsmen from the automotive school are learning fractions. "Now we have six-eighths," says the teacher, a Peace Corps veteran named Jean Bottcher. "How many sixteenths are there in six-eighths?" (Miss Bottcher is one of a number of women instructors at Kilmer. On the wall in her classroom someone has hung the sign: BE A GENTLEMAN. THERE IS A LADY PRESENT.) She moves to a table where a young man is having trouble. "By the end of the week," she tells him, "you'll understand it perfectly. Just let a little time go by."

There is no sense of schedule here, no pressure on students to master something by a certain date or be considered failures. But neither are there any fun-and-games. "The idea of discipline has to be there," Miss Bottcher says. Each Corpsman moves at his own pace: If he can read above the eighth grade level, he is encouraged to work full time for his high school equivalency diploma; if he is not up to fourth grade level, he is then enrolled in intensive remedial work. . . .

To a significant degree, despite the emphasis on literacy, Kilmer's vocational programs overshadow the academic. The Corpsmen are there to learn a trade; they were defeated by academics in the first place, and they can therefore understand the relevance of a lathe or socket wrench far more easily than they can warm up to a problem in long division. Tooling a machine part to the required dimensions has about it an immediacy and an honesty that escapes the more bookish kinds of enterprise. . . .

But the shop work, no matter how it builds confidence, is not as crucial at Kilmer as the program called Guided Group Interaction (GGI), the daily meeting conducted in each of the dormitories. GGI is part discipline ("social control"), part morale booster, and, though not so intended, part therapy. Formally GGI is described as an effort to use peer group influence to build responsibility—the responsibility each man must assume for himself and for the group. "This is our real social-studies program," said Grady. "Instead of teaching them a health course, teach them to clean up after shaving. Or teach them what it means to hurt somebody." . . .

Any group of Corpsmen includes the boisterous, the lonely, the defeated. Some assume an early tone of bravado; others rarely speak at all. A good many, despite their poor homes, become homesick and want to leave in the first few days; some go AWOL (because of Kilmer's proximity to the New York area, its AWOL statistics are high); others quit before they complete a program. The average stay at Kilmer is between seven and eight months, but of those Corpsmen who begin, fewer than half complete their training course and graduate.

"What we're fighting for is time," said Arthur Aronoff, one of the Center's counselors, "If we can bring them through six weeks, we've got it made." . . .

Among other things, the Job Corps experience seems to suggest that hitching education to tangible rewards—jobs, money, success—may be more promising than the symbolic rewards of grades and diplomas. . . .

The major task of the Job Corps is not the teaching of skills (most of which merely qualify the graduate to become an apprentice in his trade) but the thing . . . called "social development." In one sense, this simply means generating an environment in which the Corpsmen will again learn to trust adults and the larger world and to communicate with them. In another, it means, as an outside critic remarked, "teaching the kids to make demands of society." Some of the Corps leaders at Kilmer sound like the Chamber of Commerce: They are learning a trade, they will get a job when they finish, they believe in what they do. Whether they really believe it or are only putting it on—giving the Man back what he told them—is another question. Significantly, however, a number plan to go into social work, and several Kilmer alumni are already on the staff.

"I think," said Grady, who used to be the assistant superintendent of schools in Wayne, New Jersey, "that most of the kids here feel someone's trying to help. They know there's no elite, no academic shock troops. This is the first fifty-two card game they've ever been in."

**What Do You Think?**

Does the Job Corps offer an effective way of drawing alienated individuals back into the main stream of society? Why or why not?

## 11. TO SAVE THE LIFE OF "I" *

*This final reading offers a novel proposal for child-rearing, which the author believes would help to build inner strength in succeeding generations. Ask yourself, as you read, how you might be different were you to have grown up in the "Chamber" described in the article.*

To want to be very good, to live at one's fullest powers, is fundamentally healthy. It is a choice . . . that is self-imposed and self-directed. To want to be better than others, to want to be something or have something that others are and have is a compulsion fed by matters outside of yourself. The scale is always relative: not a good job, but a better job; not a good house, but a better house; not good marks, but better marks; not a good car, but a better car. The satisfactions of adequacy are forever denied.

This business of measuring yourself by others means, of course, that you are never away from others, that you move with the crowd. The closer people huddle together, the more ferocious the competition. Whether it is neat suburban houses, cheek by jowl, and the immediate comparisons of lawn and lamp and car and curtain, or the strip-lit mazes of offices in skyscrapers, there is no escape into that solitude in which a man can determine what is right and good for him rather than how others rate him.

The race starts with the children. With no immunity to the infection in the air, they start in the first grade measuring themselves—and being measured—against others. The little girl's clothes, the little boy's tests, the birthday parties, the allowances, the toys—they must never fall behind the accepted standards, for they are evidence of the worth of their families, their father's jobs, their mother's layer cakes, their make of car. The small minds are cluttered from the age of six with the values of others—values which bear little relation to their own private capacities, needs, and desires. Everything that happens to them is channelled towards one imperative end: that they be successes. For a girl this means that

* Reprinted by permission of Harold Ober Associates Incorporated. Copyright ©
1964 by Marya Mannes.

she must be popular and preferably married—to the right boy, of course—before she is twenty. For a boy, it means that he must enter the right college, get the right job, and marry the right girl by the time he is twenty-four—at the latest. That it is not possible for half the population to achieve these golden goals is considered irrelevant; until new books and articles and studies count the cost of this irrelevance in terms of student-breakdowns, adult psychoses, and a host of human aberrations ranging from destructive college riots to drugs and perversions, to any of the many violent manifestations of people under stress. For every five well-adjusted and smoothly functioning Americans, there are two who never had the chance to discover themselves. It may well be because they have never been alone with themselves. The great omission in American life is solitude; not loneliness, for this is an alienation that thrives most in the midst of crowds, but that zone of time and space free from outside pressure which is the incubator of the spirit.

If this is a valid assumption, we might then seriously consider steps to provide this incubation for our children. Thanks largely to the late President Kennedy, we have been made aware at last of the physical deficiencies of our over-comfortable young: their flabby muscles, their unused legs, their soft, sweet, chewless diets.

But what about the young souls? I myself have long wanted to see a specific program of spiritual fitness initiated in the nation. It would have nothing to do with the over-inflated and emotionally clouded issue of school prayers (what can a swiftly mumbled sequence of words once a day do for a child's illumination?)—but would establish at the outset, as a human need and norm, that each child would be left entirely alone every day for a period ranging from one hour, at the age of four, say, to three hours by the time he or she is sixteen.

Let it be said at once that this is easier said than done, for it requires two conditions: relatively small families and some extra space. In the long term, however, both are prime essentials for the survival of civilized man, and neither can be achieved without the other. Our unchecked proliferation, since it daily diminishes space, is the single greatest obstacle to the human fulfillment for which this degree of solitude is designed. For its end product is insufficiency: not being equipped to stand alone, the individual joins the crowd. Only by developing a race of individuals, therefore, capable of a high degree of sufficiency can we avert the ultimate disaster: the race of the rats toward extinction by numbers.

So let those of us who can afford it take this first step: a space in the home where each child not only can—but must—be alone for a specified time every day of his life.

What would be in this room? Let's first establish what would *not* be in it. There would be no television set, no radio, and probably no record-changer. These would be available in the living room for use at parental discretion or in parental absence. But in the Chamber—as we might call it—there would be no pacifiers, no entertainers, no crutches, no substitutions for imagination and effort. There would be no comic books, and a bare minimum of pre-school readers or "kiddy-books."

There would, however, be a lot of other things: several musical instruments, from the primitive (triangle, drum, or cymbal) to recorder to violin or piano; sheet music and instruction manuals; painting, drawing, and construction material; a microscope and slides; and every kind of book, from dictionaries to novels, from histories to poems, from art reproductions to series on the natural and physical sciences. That many of these would continue to be a step ahead of the child's knowledge at every stage of his growth is deliberate, for there is abundant evidence that many children are capable of understanding far more than is normally expected of them. As for the others, they would be free to take what they could of what the Chamber contained at their own speed and without outside pressures or measurements. This would be their world entirely, never shadowed by expectations of success or evidences of failure.

Now the Chamber holds obvious hazards. The first would be an initial resistance on the part of the child to being left alone without adult attention: a resistance shared by young mothers long brainwashed into believing that their constant presence is a token of loving care. The harassed and practical parent of three young offspring would furthermore view with alarm the upkeep of the room and its contents and the repair of objects mauled by small fingers ignorant of their proper use. No single family, in fact, could hope to win the battle of the Chamber alone. Ironically enough, it would have to become not only socially acceptable to many but in itself a sort of status symbol. Regularity, consistency, habit—these could in time overcome the initial resistances.

But not for all children. The Chamber, in fact, would become a most valuable determinant of inner stability, of mental and spiritual health. The child without either would soon find the Chamber intolerable and fight it with all his might. This resistance might take the form either of destructiveness, making a shambles of the room and its contents; or of total passivity: a sort of sit-down strike of mindless doodling. Either would alert any sensible parent to psychological trouble that demanded swift attention. For by this time—five—ten—twenty years from now?— it will hopefully have become apparent that adjustment to self and not to others is the index of the whole human being. To be at peace with self, to find company and nourishment in self—this would be the text of the free and productive psyche.

As it is now, though, lack of this sufficiency can be masked for many years in the guise of gregariousness. Under given stresses later in life the popular girl, never without dates or beaux or group activities, is more likely to break than the girl accustomed to private pursuits and frequent solitudes. And the popular boy, the regular guy, the leader, the successful competitor in school and college and job and community may conceal an inner vacuum incapable of sustaining him in times of real stress. His kind—succumbing in his forties—fills the obituary pages.

The function of the Chamber, then, would be to equip girl or boy for life with inner resources to withstand the external assaults of a competitive society. It would make them aware of what they are and what they want instead of what others think they should be and should have. What's more, this adjustment to self would in the end lead to—and not preclude—a genuine adjustment to others. And by genuine I mean relationships sought not for social approval or status, but for personal need. There is a world of difference between the mass gregariousness which has for so long been the admired hallmark of American "friendliness" ("Hi, fella," to everyone and anyone) and the real, deep, sustained emotions of friendship. The graduates of the Chamber would learn to choose between the glad hand and the open heart.

Those who believe this concept of the Chamber not only far-fetched but impracticable might find some evidence of its validity in the lives of great human beings, past and present. In the past, to be sure, the Chamber did not have to be fabricated; it was more often a fact of life in the small societies and rural enclaves of an earlier and infinitely smaller world. For the privileged, there was the empty library or the small study or the enclosed garden. For the poor, there was still the sanctuary of surrounding nature, the banks of rivers, or the courtyards of towns. There were many places where a child could wander alone and build his world. And more often than not, it was such children who built the best of our world.

But today, this refuge is less and less attainable, let alone acknowledged as desirable. It would have to be imposed and preserved as a deliberate act: a measure established for the spiritual survival of a people, designed for the preservation of the individual and for the kind of democracy which cannot exist without him.

\*     \*     \*     \*     \*

The view from the Chamber is one of life, not death; and the profit—the preservation of an inviolate core called "I"—far greater a goal than getting ahead of "Them."

You might say that the child in the Chamber and the astronaut in his capsule are not far apart. In solitude, our astronauts discover outer space; in isolation, our groundlings find their stars. With these to steer by, the race—to obliteration—can be left to the rats.

---

**What Do You Think?**

1.  Why do you think the writer calls her article, "To Save the Life of 'I' "?

2.   At one point, the writer distinguishes between solitude and loneliness. Indicate what you believe to be the difference between the two and give several examples of each.

## ACTIVITIES FOR INVOLVEMENT

1.   Many of the proposals for dealing with alienation involve major changes in the way our society is "set up." Invite a number of people from your community (e.g., a parent, a policeman, a dropout, a social worker, a minister, a lawyer, a teacher, your principal, etc.) to participate in a panel discussion on the topic, "Obstacles to a concerted effort to combat alienation in America today." Then invite a number of other people (including class members) to participate in a panel discussion on "Opportunities for action in combatting alienation in America today."

2.   There are probably a number of people in your community who have participated in some form of volunteer program to help eliminate social ills. Make arrangements for one or more such persons to speak to the class on their experiences. Do they advocate it as one means of dealing with alienation? Why or why not? You may, after exploring the matter further, want to see if you can arrange to participate in one of these programs yourself.

3.   Find out what the citizen liability laws are in your state and report to your class. If you believe Louis Nizer's proposal for new "Good Samaritan" laws is a good one, write a letter to your state representative or state senator outlining the proposal and urging his support. If you oppose the proposal, write a letter setting forth the reasons for your opposition.

4.   The topics in this chapter provide a number of opportunities for inviting speakers to your class. You might, for example, invite:

    a.   A local political leader to speak on participatory democracy, and its relationship (if any) to alienation.

    b.   A prominent member of the Negro community to speak on his view of "Black Power," and its relationship (if any) to alienation.

    c.   A local businessman to discuss business involvement in ghetto self-help efforts and its relationship (if any) to alienation.

There are other possibilities that might suggest themselves to you. Pick one or more and follow through on it.

5.   See if you can get your student council to sponsor a Saturday conference for parents, teachers, and young people on "The role of students in school and society," and offer to provide leadership in organizing the conference. Be sure to invite "keynote" speakers representing a variety of points of view. Organize discussion groups in such a way as to encourage an interchange of ideas among the three groups.

6.   If interested, several members of your class might prepare a brief play in which they portray how life might be different for some alienated persons *after* they had dealt effectively with their alienation or with the conditions that had led to it.

# BIBLIOGRAPHY
## For Further Study

## Books

AUDEN, W. H. · *The Age of Anxiety* · New York, N. Y.: Random House, Inc., 1947.

BETTELHEIM, BRUNO · *The Informed Heart: Autonomy in a Mass Age* · Glencoe, Ill.: Free Press, 1960.

DOBRINER, WILLIAM (ed.) · *The Suburban Community* · New York, N. Y.: Putnam's, 1958.

ELIOT, T. S. · "The Hollow Men," in *Collected Poems, 1909–1962* · New York, N. Y.: Harcourt, Brace & World, 1963.

HARRINGTON, ALAN · *Life in the Crystal Palace* · New York, N. Y.: Alfred A. Knopf, Inc., 1959.

IBSEN, HENRIK · *A Doll's House,* in *Ibsen,* translated and edited by J. W. McFarlane · New York, N. Y.: Oxford University Press, 1960.

KAFKA, FRANZ · *The Castle* · New York, N. Y.: Modern Library.

MILLER, ARTHUR · *Death of a Salesman,* in *Collected Plays* · New York, N. Y.: Viking Press, Inc., 1957.

MILLS, C. WRIGHT · *White Collar* · New York, N. Y.: Oxford University Press, 1956.

MOUSTAKAS, CLARK · *Loneliness* · Englewood Cliffs, N. J.: Prentice-Hall, Inc., 1961.

RICE, ELMER · *The Adding Machine,* in *Seven Plays* · New York, N. Y.: Viking Press, Inc., 1950.

WILSON, COLIN · *The Outsider* · Boston, Mass.: Houghton Mifflin, 1956.

WOOD, MARGARET · *Paths of Loneliness* · New York, N. Y.: Columbia Univ. Press, 1960.

## Paperback Books

BERNE, ERIC · *Games People Play* · New York, N. Y.: Dell Paperbacks.

CAMUS, ALBERT · *The Fall* · New York, N. Y.: Vintage Books.

CAMUS, ALBERT · *The Stranger* · New York, N. Y.: Vintage Books.

CLEAVER, ELDRIDGE · *Soul on Ice* · New York, N. Y.: Delta Books.

DE BEAUVOIR, SIMONE · *The Second Sex* · New York, N. Y.: Bantam Books.

FRANKL, VIKTOR · *Man's Search for Meaning* · New York, N. Y.: Washington Square Press.

FRIEDENBERG, EDGAR Z. · *The Vanishing Adolescent* · New York, N. Y.: Dell Paperbacks.

FROMM, ERICH · *Escape from Freedom* · New York, N. Y.: Fawcett World Library.

GOODMAN, PAUL · *Growing Up Absurd* · New York, N. Y.: Vintage Books.

HOFFER, ERIC · *The True Believer* · New York, N. Y.: Mentor Books.

KAZAN, ELIA · *The Arrangement* · New York, N. Y.: Avon Books.

REISMAN, DAVID · *The Lonely Crowd* · New Haven, Conn.: Yale University Press.

RILKE, RAINER MARIA · *Duino Elegies* · Los Angeles, Cal.: University of California Press.

SILBERMAN, CHARLES E. · *Crisis in Black and White* · New York, N. Y.: Vintage Books.

WHYTE, WILLIAM H., JR. · *The Organization Man* · Garden City, New York: Doubleday Anchor Books.

WILSON, SLOAN · *The Man in the Grey Flannel Suit* · New York, N. Y.: Pocketbooks, Inc.

## Articles

ANDERS, GUNTHER · "Reflections on the H-Bomb," *Dissent,* Spring 1956.

BERGER, MONROE · "The Black Muslims," *Horizon,* January 1964.

BETTELHEIM, BRUNO · "Joey: A Mechanical Boy," *Scientific American,* March 1959.

BINGER, CARL · "The Pressures on College Girls Today," *The Atlantic Monthly,* February 1961.

BRZEZINSKI, ZBIGNIEW · "The American Transition," *The New Republic,* December 23, 1967.

DUBERMAN, MARTIN · "On Misunderstanding Student Rebels," *The Atlantic Monthly,* November 1968.

FRIEDAN, BETTY · "Women Are People, Too," *Good Housekeeping,* September 1960.

HALLECK, S. L. · "Hypotheses of Student Unrest," *Phi Delta Kappan,* September 1968.

KENISTON, KENNETH · "Alienation and the Decline of Utopia," *American Scholar,* Spring 1960.

MAILER, NORMAN · "The White Negro," *Dissent,* Summer 1957.

MUSGROVE, FRANK · "The Adolescent Ghetto," *The Nation,* September 21, 1964.

ROBBINS, JHAN, and JUNE ROBBINS · "Why Young Mothers Feel Trapped," *Redbook,* September 1960.

SIGAL, CLANCY · "Short Talk with a Fascist Beast," *New Statesman,* October 4, 1958.

SILVERMAN, CHARLES E. · "Up from Apathy—The Woodlawn Experiment," *Commentary,* May 1964.

WALD, GEORGE · "A Generation in Search of a Future," Speech made March 4, 1969, at Massachusetts Institute of Technology, printed in part in "The Talk of the Town," *The New Yorker,* March 22, 1969.

## Films, Filmstrips, Tapes

*Automation* (84 min; B/W; CBS "See It Now" series) · Explores the many problems connected with the revolutionary development of automation and shows automation at work in dozens of industries.

*Beyond Three Doors* \* (26 min; color) · Takes you behind the doors of three citizens, each of whom sets out to solve different problems in his community (water pollution, a new highway, and a local election). The over-all lessons of citizen participation for better government are more important that the issues themselves.

*Children Without* \* (29 min; B/W) · Documents the desperate conditions under which children grow up in the inner city and the efforts of education to break the cycle.

*Cities: How They Grow* \* (10 min; B/W) · Explains factors which determine location and growth of cities. Shows the general trend toward organization throughout the U. S. Various types of cities and city plans are presented. Factors involved in the decentralization of city planning are suggested.

*Harvest of Shame* \* (54 min; B/W) · Depicts the plight of migratory workers who harvest America's crops. On-the-scene reports from Florida, Georgia, Virginia, New Jersey, New York, Michigan, and California show crowded, unsanitary huts and long work hours for little pay.

*Experimental Studies in the Social Climate of Groups* \* (30 min; B/W) · Shows behavior of boys organized in clubs run on democratic principles, as an autocracy, and as a laissez-faire group. Shows responses when groups are changed from one type to another.

*New Lives for Old* \* (20 min; B/W) · The story of striking change experienced in a 25-year period by the Manus people of the Admiralty Islands and the society's adaptation to a new way of life.

*An American Comes Home* † (Tape; 15 min; New Frontiers of Human Freedom Series) · Dramatization of discrimination in a resort. Features Faye Emerson.

---

\* Available from Audio-Visual Center, University of Maine, Orono, Maine 04473.
† Available from Audio-Visual Instruction, Division of Continuing Education, Coliseum 131, Corvallis, Oregon 97331.

*These Small Things* † (Tape; 15 min; New Frontiers of Human Freedom Series) · Dramatization of discrimination in housing. Features Mac-Donald Carey.

*With Malice Toward All* † (Tape; 15 min; New Frontiers of Human Freedom Series) · Detective story dealing with group hatred. Features Staats Cotsworth.

*You Are Not Alone* † (Tape; 30 min; Ways of Mankind Series) · People as members, creators, and products of groups. Each person is a member of many groups. None is a separate individual.

*Man on the Assembly Line* † (27 min; B/W) · Examines the problem of the assembly line worker; suggests that modern industrial society must find solutions to the stresses resulting from assembly line production methods.

*Of Men and Machines* † (29 min; B/W) · Experiments in engineering psychology on the relationship between men and machines; How the information gained from research has led to redesigning of equipment to fit human capabilities.

*Our Invisible Committees* † (25 min; B/W) · How personal and outside pressures affect the individual in his actions with groups.

*City: Heaven and Hell* † (28 min; B/W) · Creative and destructive forces affecting city in history; elements influencing the creation of the first cities; forces threatening to destroy the city.

*City as Man's Home* † (28 min; B/W) · How slums, giant public housing complexes, mass suburbs, and bleak luxury apartments contribute to the lowering of communal standards of living while personal standards of living are rising. What cities can do to raise the communal standard of living.

*Boredom at Work: The Empty Life* † (23 min; B/W) · Uses dramatization of several instances to demonstrate the problem of boredom and its effect on the individual.

*Boredom at Work: The Search for Zest* † (11 min; B/W) · How time can be used "constructively" through a self-planned program of activities both interesting and educational.

*Nation of Spoilers* † (11 min; color) · Common kinds of vandalism in scenic areas and on public property. Prevalence of litter. Public responsibility in these areas.

*Co-operation, Competition, and Conflict* † (9 min; B/W) · The facets of co-operation, competition, and conflict in a small town, as they affect social interaction in daily activities.

*Alcohol and Social Responsibility Series* ‡ · This series of tapes deals with the nature and implications of alcoholism as a social problem. Each of the following tapes is fifteen minutes long.

---

† Available from Audio-Visual Instruction, Division of Continuing Education, Coliseum 131, Corvallis, Oregon 97331.

‡ Available from National Center for Audio Tapes, Bureau of Audio-Visual Instruction, Stadium Building Room 320, University of Colorado, Boulder, Colorado 80302.

1. *Alcoholic, Skid Row, Rejection.*
2. *Alcoholism as a Social Disorder.*
3. *Reports on Alcoholism and Social Responsibility.*

*Automation Series* ‡ · This series of tapes describes impact of automation on American society. The selections listed below focus on the psychological and social effects of automation. Each is thirty minutes long.

1. *The New Industrial Revolution.*
2. *Impact of Automation in the Office.*
3. *Psychological Adjustments to Automation.*
4. *The Challenge of Automation for Labor.*

*Resolved: That Beatniks Are a Symptom of Moral Decadence* ‡ (Tape; 30 min) · A debate exploring various alternative approaches to the phenomenon of the beatnik or hippie culture in America.

*University of Chicago Roundtable: Political Apathy in America* ‡ (Tape; 30 min) · A dramatic discussion of the causes, nature, and consequences of political apathy on the political and social life of this country.

*Some of My Best Friends* ‡ (Tape; 15 min) · Program of discussion with dramatizations of actual cases of discrimination and anti-Semitism in America.

*Pall Over America* (Film; 15 min; B/W; Nat'l Medical A-V Center, Film Distribution, Chamblee, Georgia 30005) · A summary of the air pollution problem, showing principal sources of dirty air, including industrial operations, burning dumps, motor vehicles, and combustion of fossil fuels.

*Skid Row—The Homeless Man* (Film; 30 min; B/W; Redevelopment Authority, City of Philadelphia, Public Information Office, City Hall Annex, Philadelphia, Pa. 19107) · Deals with work being done to rehabilitate men on skid row.

*Production 5118* § (Filmstrip; 28 min; sound) · Dramatizes incidents to provoke discussion of the problems of human communication: of understanding oneself, of being understood, of understanding others.

*No Reason to Stay* § (Film; 28 min; B/W) · Dramatizes dilemma faced by an able high school student who comes to feel that school is repressive, degrading, and irrelevant to his life.

*Capitalism and Democracy* § (Tape; 60 min) · Raises question as to whether capitalism is inherently undemocratic because of the way in which economic decisions are made.

*The Elite and the Electorate* (Tape; 60 min) · A discussion of whether democracy by the people is possible in view of the functions of the executive and legislative branches of the federal government, especially in the area of foreign policy.

---

‡ Available from National Center for Audio Tapes, Bureau of Audio-Visual Instruction, Stadium Building Room 320, University of Colorado, Boulder, Colorado 80302.
§ Available from A-V Utilization Center, 5448 Cass Ave., Wayne State University, Detroit, Michigan 48202.

*Portrait of the Inner City* (Film; 17 min; B/W) · Kaleidoscopic views of streets, schools, and living quarters of the inner city slums of a large urban community in the U. S. Positive as well as negative aspects of poverty-striken areas. From point of view of young Tommy Knight as he grows up in this environment.

*Portrait of a Disadvantaged Child* (Film; 16 min; B/W) · A day in the life of a slum child. The problems, needs, and strengths of an inner city boy.